Hans Christian Andersen
in China

Hans Christian Andersen in China

Edited by
Johs. Nørregaard Frandsen
Sun Jian
Torben Grøngaard Jeppesen

University Press of Southern Denmark 2014

Publications from the Hans Christian Andersen Center
Volume 2: *Hans Christian Andersen in China*

In cooperation with Fudan University, Shanghai
Referring to the Fudan University Key-Project 2011RWXKZD026

University of Southern Denmark Studies in
Scandinavian Languages and Literatures vol. 120

Published by University Press of Southern Denmark
© The authors and University Press of Southern Denmark

Cover illustration: Christmas Tree Ornament. Front and back. 1850.
By Hans Christian Andersen
Odense City Museums/Hans Christian Andersen Museum

Cover design: Donald Jensen, Unisats
Layout and Print: Narayana Press

Printed in Denmark 2014
ISBN 978 87 7674 820 3

University Press of Southern Denmark
Campusvej 55
DK-5230 Odense M
www.universitypress.dk

Distribution in the United States and Canada:
International Specialized Book Services
5804 NE Hassalo Street
Portland, OR 97213-3644 USA
www.isbs.com

Distribution in the United Kingdom:
Gazelle Book Services Ltd.
White Cross Mills, Hightown,
Lancaster, Lancashire
LA1 4XS
UK
www.gazellebookservices.co.uk

Table of Contents

Foreword   7
By Her Majesty Queen Margrethe II of Denmark

Preface   9
Johs. Nørregaard Frandsen, Sun Jian, and Torben Grøngaard Jeppesen

Hans Christian Andersen and his Chinese Dreams   13
Johs. Nørregaard Frandsen

The Reception of Hans Christian Andersen on Campus   29
Sun Jian

Ransoming Andersen   39
China's Reception of Hans Christian Andersen
and the Dilemma of its Andersen Studies
Lu Li'an

Hans Christian Andersen in China   75
An Overview
Ye Rulan

When Heritage Tourism goes Glocal   95
The Little Mermaid in Shanghai
Anne Klara Bom

Chinese Interpretations of Andersen's Fairy Tales   117
Li Hongye

A Discussion on Political Appropriation of Andersen's   123
Fairy Tales in China
Zhu Jianxin

Fantasy, Irony, and Autonomy A Feminist Transcoding of "The Little Mermaid" *Wang Aiping*	133
Hans Christian Andersen and the Arabesque *Jacob Bøggild*	147
Gender, Body, and Space A Spatial Analysis of "The Little Mermaid" *Chen Liang*	155
Paper Cutting A Universal Language of Hans Christian Andersen *Ye Rulan*	167
References	179
Bio Notes	191

Foreword
By Her Majesty Queen Margrethe II of Denmark

Hans Christian Andersen's great art arose out of his imaginative and creative use of what was close at hand and the things around him. He could make a darning needle or a tea pot become a living 'human' personality, or let his imagination fly over the hills and far away in a trunk – even all the way to China. All of his characters, objects, persons and fantastic creatures became live personalities that we can follow and empathize with. He always expressed himself in a poetic yet direct language that still goes straight to our hearts, no matter where in the world our home is, and takes us into the world of Fairy tale.

Hans Christian Andersen grew up in straitened circumstances in the city of Odense in Denmark, but became both known and loved in many countries during his own lifetime. It is with great pride that we Danes discover that Hans Christian Andersen's oeuvre and his art are natural doorways to conversation and understanding between people around the world. Hans Christian Andersen tells stories that are universally relevant drawing all of us into the realm of fairy tale and fantasy. He is beloved in the whole world, and his fairy tales have thereby become the whole world's fairy tales.

In my family, we have always had a very close relationship to Hans Christian Andersen's work, and it has been profoundly enriching to have had the opportunity to work with – and in – his universe. It gives me the greatest pleasure and gratification to contribute to the spreading of knowledge about Hans Christian Andersen, whose fairy tales I myself came to know as a child when my father read them aloud to me.

It is therefore a source of joy that this book about Hans Christian Andersen and his great importance in China sees the light of day. A unique collaboration between Chinese and Danish researchers has resulted in a book that contributes to building yet another bridge between Danish and Chinese culture – as well as between people in the world.

Preface

As a boy, the writer and teller of fairy tales Hans Christian Andersen (1805-1875) dreamt about China and about a fairytale Chinese prince who was going to appear on the scene and grant him happiness, recognition, and wealth. Hans Christian Andersen never got to visit China in his lifetime. Back then, the sheer physical distance between China and Europe was insurmountable for most people, but Andersen's dreams, fairy tales and other tales have made that long journey from Denmark to China.

Today, Hans Christian Andersen is known, admired and read throughout the world. In China he means something quite special as a teller of fairy tales whom most people are familiar with from their early childhood. That is also the case in Denmark, where Andersen's fairy tales and characters have long since become a part of the everyday language and the Danish cultural heritage, passed on from one generation to the next. Hans Christian Andersen's fairy tales thus form a kind of cultural bridge between the peoples of China and Denmark, for despite different languages, traditions and cultures we can meet in the light of Andersen's wise, philosophical and warm-hearted stories.

In the summer of 2010, Professor Sun Jian from Fudan University in Shanghai met up with Professor Johs. Nørregaard Frandsen from the University of Southern Denmark (SDU) in Odense, at the Nordic Centre of Fudan. Via mail and with the help of the proficient staff at the Nordic Centre, a meeting had been arranged for the two professors to exchange experiences about Hans Christian Andersen in Denmark and China respectively. This proved to be a fruitful meeting, where – among other things – collaboration was agreed between research teams on Hans Christian Andersen's Global Significance.

As early as autumn 2011, we held our first workshop on Andersen's cultural and literary significance at the Nordic Centre, which organized a delightful seminar. Researchers from Fudan, SDU and Odense City Museums/Hans Christian Andersen Museum took part. These were unforgettable days during which we also discussed the reading of Andersen by young people. We had asked young Chinese students and young Danish students to write short essays about their reading of and reaction to certain selected fairy tales by Andersen. This provided a first, splendid insight into similarities and differences between the way young Danes and Chinese read Andersen.

Since then, researchers from Fudan University, SDU and Odense City Museums have held workshops in Odense as well as Shanghai. The first step, taken on a lovely autumn day in 2011, formed the basis for meetings, conversations, and a fantastic collaboration of the kind that helps to advance and develop research.

The present book is the first major result of this collaboration. Naturally, it had to have the title *Hans Christian Andersen in China*. The papers have been written by Chinese and Danish researchers, each of whom has delved down and excavated a piece of archaeology about Andersen and his importance in China.

The book pinpoints and analyses Andersen's considerable significance as a teller of fairy tales and a cultural icon in modern China. It furthermore contains analyses of the reception of Andersen from the time the first fairy tales were translated into Chinese in the second decade of the 20th century. Other papers depict the cultural and literary history of cause and effect that one has to be familiar with to understand Hans Christian Andersen's great importance in China today. Two papers deal in depth with the political context which is also a very important aspect of, and an essential framework for, Andersen's literary significance and widespread popular appeal. One paper deals with Hans Christian Andersen's papercuts and draws comparisons with traditional Chinese paper cutting. Finally, there are contributions that analyse aesthetical and narrational aspects of Andersen's fairy tales.

We – the editors – feel we have made up a bouquet of various academic flowers, all of which have something special in mind: to shed light on Hans Christian Andersen in China. We wish our readers a pleasant journey through the papers and essays in the book.

The editors would like to express their gratitude to Her Majesty Queen Margrethe II of Denmark, who has graciously contributed with a greeting in the form of a Foreword. We would also like to thank The Hans Christian Andersen Foundation in Odense, which has provided financial support for the printing and publishing of the book. Many thanks also to the University Press of Southern Denmark and – not least – to colleagues and staff whose efforts have made this book possible.

Johs. Nørregaard Frandsen
Sun Jian
Torben Grøngaard Jeppesen

Hans Christian Andersen and his Chinese Dreams

Johs. Nørregaard Frandsen
Professor, Head of the Hans Christian Andersen Center,
University of Southern Denmark

The Danish writer Hans Christian Andersen (1805-75) is known and famous for his fairy tales and stories throughout the world. He also wrote novels, plays, poems, and travel books. But it is particularly his fairy tales and short stories, such as "The Little Mermaid", "The Ugly Duckling", "The Match-Stick Girl", "The Emperor's New Clothes", "The Tinder-Box", "The Swineherd", "Thumbelina", "The Nightingale", "The Princess and the Pea", and "The Story of a Mother", that are read, told and re-told everywhere in the world.

Today, there are versions of Andersen's fairy tales in more than 150 languages, and it is fantastic to think that his stories are read by schoolchildren in such countries as Denmark, China, The Philippines, Korea, USA, Australia, Brazil, South Africa, Mali, Spain, France, Germany, Italy, Romania, and Russia. Schoolchildren in China read a number of his fairy tales as part of their fixed curriculum, for in China Hans Christian Andersen is considered to be an important author who writes about true feelings and the truth of feelings. In that way, Hans Christian Andersen and his fairy tales are both a Danish and global cultural heritage, and via his artistic universe dialogue can be created with people out in the world who have a heart and feelings (Frandsen, "Writer of Tales" 2).

Journey to Shanghai 2010

The little mermaid is beautiful, enchanting, seductive, inscrutable. The warm rays of the sun shine on her reddish and green bronze skin, on her thighs, the rounded breasts and her plaited hair as well as on the large granite stone on which she has sat with her tail since 1913. The little mermaid is among the best-known of Andersen's literary figures.

For many decades she has also been one of Denmark's greatest tourist icons – a lovely bronze statue at the water's edge on Langelinie and the Sound near Copenhagen Harbour. She was created by the Danish sculptor Edvard Eriksen in 1913, having been commissioned by the owner of the Carlsberg brewery, brewer Carl Jacobsen, who at that time was Denmark's greatest patron of the arts. In 2010, the little mermaid left the windy Langelinie with special permission from the Municipality of Copenhagen, which owns her, and now for the first time ever she was about to travel outside Denmark! She travelled all the way to China on her stone. Admittedly, she did not travel as a spirit of the air, as could have been expected of Andersen's little mermaid, but was carefully transported out here by Scandinavian Airlines in a Boeing 747 (Bom).

I found myself in her company on a beautiful sunny day in 2010 in the middle of Shanghai at the mouth of the Yangtze, down by the banks of the tributary Hangpu, which flows through the city, with The Bund on one side and Pudong on the other. Here the mermaid sat as a natural focal point in the Danish architect Bjarke Ingels' white fairy tale of a snail's shell that was Denmark's official pavilion at the world exposition 2010. The little mermaid is portrayed at the point where the transformation of fish's tail to feet is taking place. She portrays transformation, but also the retention of the fame that characterizes Hans Christian Andersen's art and life's work. She is a national icon, but at the same time a global symbol. She has no clothes on, but there is nobody, as in "The Emperor's New Clothes" who accuses her of not being able to discharge her duties, for she is a creature of fairy tale and created for the sake of fairy tale. The visitors at EXPO 2010 worshipped her and pawed over her amphibious body with the optical eyes of their cameras. More than eight million people visited her in the pavilion, which was next to Pippi Longstocking's Villa Villakulla and Thorbjørn Egner's Cardamom Town. The Nordic countries seem to agree on the importance of the fairy tale. Shanghai thundered like the enormous metropolis it is, but the little mermaid said nothing. It is her fate and her nature not to say anything and to be unable to say anything (Wang Aiping; Chen Liang; Bøggild).

Hans Christian Andersen would have loved EXPO 2010, as he loved La Exposition Universelle on the Champ de Mars in Paris in 1867, which he depicted in the tale "The Dryad" from 1868. He would have loved the mermaid's journey and perhaps have thought that she ended up not floating into God's kingdom but into the middle kingdom of the fairy tale. She had to give up the most valuable thing she owned and yet fail to gain the dearest thing she wished for. So she sits there, silent and inscrutable on her stone. She pays the price for wanting so whole-heartedly her dream of happiness. She pays the price for breaking the mould, her reckless rise towards what is highest.

The enchanting mermaid had to endure so much. She was born of Andersen's pen and published in 1837 in *Eventyr, fortalte for Børn. Første Samling. Tredie Hefte* (Tales Told for Children. Book Three). From birth she was among the more complex of Andersen's characters. Good heavens! Couldn't she just have been content with being the youngest of the sea-king's six daughters down there in the ocean kingdom, where carefree beauty and weightless well-being gleam in the oceanic halls? Then she could have lived 300 carefree years! But no! She longed, and longing is her most important characteristic. As a 15-year-old mermaid she was granted, as was customary among sea-folk, a glimpse above and out across the surface of the water – and thereby into the unfamiliar world where humans live. The world she had dreamt of and formed images of in her own small garden near her father's palace on the sea-bed, with flowers as the sun and a marble statue of a human boy.

To long for something has its price, and the little mermaid had to hand over her voice, which is the sea's loveliest and the siren's attribute. That is the security the sea-witch demands for starting the transformation from the mermaid's tail into human legs. The mermaid must give up herself in order to become the one she even so can never completely become. She gives up her voice to say what now can never be said to the person who therefore will never be able to hear it. The dance, the graceful lightness of the body, the deepness of the eyes she still possesses, but it is all anchored in inexpressible and burning pain, because she will never be able to become what she most fervently longs for: a human being with a soul. The little mermaid pays the price for longing beyond herself, for rising up, severing all ties and patterns of living to become a human being in God's light and the spiritual dimension. Longing is the stuff humans are made of – the longing to travel, to move out into the unknown is the fairytale adventure of our age and all ages. So the infinitely beautiful but also infinitely tragic story of the mermaid who has to lose her voice to live painfully close to the one she can sing herself to happiness with is – as are all of

Andersen's fairy tales and stories – an extremely modern story about desiring to be a human being and of becoming a human being by being caught up in one's longings without ever getting them fulfilled. In his fairy tales, Andersen often tells the extremely modern story of being a restless, seeking mould-breaker who desires to arrive at his or her true self. In the fairy tale of the little mermaid, the story unfolds in such a brilliant way that the population of the world has been able to mirror itself in its longing.

Now she is sitting here as a beautiful statue and a symbol of a fantastic tale with a global impact about human beings and feelings! The little mermaid was placed on her own stone in her own water in the country of China! – This is a completely new version of the fairy tale of the little mermaid that left her own location in order to reach a new destination.

The mermaid's journey to Shanghai convinced us once again in Denmark that Hans Christian Andersen as a literary legacy is greater than anything else. Hans Christian Andersen is a great figure and particularly widespread in China, just as he is in a number of other Asian countries – and in the rest of the world for that matter. He is the best-known Dane in the world! In China, Andersen is sometimes called "An Tusheng", which can be translated as "born into a poor family" (Ye Rulan, "HCA in China"). He is not only considered a very great writer and artist in China, he is also viewed not simply as a writer of fairy tales for children but as an artistic steward of "sad stories about life and destiny". Hans Christian Andersen is not synonymous with a top hat in China but with literary work of world stature that speaks to humanity and its entire gamut of feelings.

Fantasy Moves People

Fairy tale, fantasy, and experience! These are words that often occur when one is to introduce the writer and storyteller Hans Christian Andersen. There is so much in his fairy tales that becomes visible in a new way, and that one never forgets once one has been there and seen it. The world was never the same for me again, for example, when I read these opening lines of "The Tinder-Box" ("Fyrtøiet", 1835): "There came a soldier marching down the high road–*one, two! one, two!* He had his knapsack on his back and his sword at his side as he came home from the wars." (1, 79).¹ That's exactly how a soldier moves of course – one two, one two. What do soldiers do? Well, they fight wars, and after that they long to return home. The child mind can easily understand that, and in a way the story was clear. Something had to happen, something strange, for here was a soldier ready for the unexpected: one two, one two!

It is just as obvious that the child mind opens wide when it meets the opening lines of the fairy tale "The Nightingale" ("Nattergalen", 1844): "The Emperor of China is a Chinaman, as you most likely know, and everyone around him is a Chinaman too." (1, 271). The reader is immediately allowed to enter a logical, fantastic space that a storyteller can create by determining the rules for what we are about to hear – and this then is a story all the way from the country of the Emperor of China, where everyone is a Chinaman. We are invited as readers to China. At the time of Hans Christian Andersen, China was often viewed from Denmark as being a fantastic kingdom, one that was magical, particularly perhaps because it lay so far away and was in so many ways strange and exotic compared to Denmark. So the fairy tale determines its own framework as early as in the opening lines! This is also the case in "The Swineherd" ("Svinedrengen, 1842), which begins: "Once there was a poor Prince. He had a kingdom; it was very tiny. Still it was large enough to marry upon, and on marriage his heart was set." (1, 258). Now the reader knows what is going to happen, for the prince wants to get married, and it is his wish to get married, rather than pursuit of kingdom or money, that will be the crucial thing, though he is a poor prince and his kingdom is very small. So now the listener or reader has been drawn into the rich kingdom of the fairy tale.

Hans Christian Andersen creates recognizability immediately. No one is in any doubt when meeting these words: "It was so beautiful out in the country, it was summer – the wheat fields were golden, the oats were green, and down among the green meadows the hay was stacked. There the stork minced about on his red legs, clacking away in Egyptian, which was the language his mother had taught him. Round

---

1 Concerning Andersen quotations throughout this paper, I refer to the Danish edition of his collected works, *Andersen. H. C. Andersens samlede værker*. 1-18. København: Gyldendal/Det danske Sprog- og Litteraturselskab, 2003-2007. The translations are by Jean Hersholt and are to be found on the homepage of the Hans Christian Andersen Center, Andersen.sdu.dk.

about the field and meadow lands rose vast forests, in which deep lakes lay hidden. Yes, it was indeed lovely out there in the country." (1, 284). The distant becomes so near and the near distant enough for us to see it with new eyes when Andersen takes out his palette of colours and forms in these opening lines of "The Ugly Duckling" ("Den grimme Ælling", 1843).

Hans Christian Andersen's fairy tales create a fantastic room or space that one is invited to inhabit. In these 'rooms' everything is basically so very simple, because everything has its own logic. In "The Snow Queen" ("Sneedronningen", 1845), the snow queen at one point offers the boy Kay "the whole world and a new pair of skates". (1, 328). The expression "the whole world" is quite abstract, but a pair of skates is immediately understandable to the child in us. What child wouldn't like to have a pair of new skates? And even if one has just been given the whole world – for what can one really do with that?

Andersen is amusing and he uses irony to create the small distance needed for us to be able to see ourselves and human characteristics in things – partly be amused at ourselves when we see ourselves presented as things and objects that sometimes behave in stupid ways. A ball for example can jump up and down past a swallow's nest under the eaves, for balls happen to be able to do that, also when they have a cork inside them. A ball is a ball, for it can bounce, but for Andersen and in "Sweethearts" ("Kjærestefolkene", 1844) the ball doesn't just make do with being a ball. The ball is so in love with itself and so snobbish that it doesn't notice the painted top that so much wants to be its sweetheart. It sees itself as being so fine that no one else exists for it! But the ball is also a ball, a thing, an inflated ball, and when it ends up in the roof gutter, it can lie there and go on leaking until it is unrecognizable.

Andersen's fairy tales often have to do with completely everyday things that are given life and a voice. Or with animals that are also ascribed particular roles on the stage of the fairy tale. They are assigned traits or points of view that we recognize from human life. Even so, they are not transformed into human or magic figures, as for example in Disney's universe. In Andersen, a ball is a ball and a mouse a mouse, to which a particular character or moral have been ascribed that we easily recognize from human life. This is what constitutes Andersen's wonderful irony! He creates nearness and distance to things at one and the same time.

That is also the case with the over-sophisticated princess in "The Swineherd". She becomes her own victim and thereby also the victim of Andersen's biting irony. Princesses are always fine in his work, but this one lacks inner nobility and cannot see the genuine, upright qualities of the prince. She is unmoved by the scent and beauty of real roses, as she also is by the beautiful voice of the nightingale. Because of this, she falls for cheap tricks and knick-knacks in the form of strange cooking pots and odd rattles. She prefers cheap trash to the real thing. She ends up paying a high price for this. That is the moral of the story. She does not get her prince, or her share of the kingdom, but is left standing outside.

In his fairy tales Hans Christian Andersen took up such issues as the difference between the genuine and the non-genuine, or between what has to do with the heart and that which is merely outer appearance and therefore a matter of indifference. This, among other things, is what makes Andersen such a great artist. He wants to move people! He wants to speak to the emotions and he believed that fantasy is among the strongest forces that exist. Andersen placed fantasy centre-stage and turned the child's eye view of the world into what is crucial to human existence – and in doing so he created world art.

In his tales, human nature is mirrored, for better or worse. And this makes it easy for them to cross national and social borders. All of us can find ourselves disrobed like the emperor, who is blinded by his own vanity, and when we laugh with the child, we are laughing at ourselves, because we see ourselves in the magic mirror Hans Christian Andersen holds up via his art. The world of the fairy tale is spacious, global and high-ceilinged. We were there ourselves when we were children – in that boundless, magic world. In his fairy tales we find once more the playfulness and joy in telling stories that belong to childhood, we find the existential, the universal and the universally human. We find what touches and concerns us. Humour can cross all boundaries and borders, as can longing and sorrow, love – indeed, the whole rich and complex gamut of human emotions. The fairy tale is a genre for the whole world, and the special fairy tales and stories of Hans Christian Andersen are particularly so.

A Mould-breaker

Hans Christian Andersen became a mould-breaker, one who broke with his social and cultural background. He was born in Odense on 2 April 1805 and grew up in one of the poorest precincts. He readily absorbed all the strange figures, tales, books that were read aloud to him, such as the *Arabian Nights*, heroic tales and fairy tales. He saw Spanish and French soldiers march through the town, for it was during the Napoleonic Wars. The boy also experienced horrific things such as public executions and other forms of punishment carried out on the city squares. All of this was stored in the child's imagination as colours and shadows that later developed.

When the boy left school, his mother wanted him to become a cobbler's apprentice, for he simply had to learn a trade. The boy was unwilling, however, and also had a longing to see the outside world, so he left Odense at the age of fourteen and travelled to Copenhagen, where he wanted to realize his dream of becoming famous. He loved to perform, so he wanted to be a ballet dancer, singer or actor. But alas! His voice broke, and he was also a tall, gangling figure who could never be successful on the stage. And even less become a ballet dancer. After some hard years that offered their share of humiliations, but also almost fairytale strokes of luck and in particular a stubborn, indomitable will, he managed to gain a foothold. Through good fortune and persistence he managed to make connections with influential people that took an interest in him. One of the king's advisers, Jonas Collin, took care of him and helped him. Collin and his home became the bastion without which Hans Christian would never have made his mark. He also regarded the Collin's house as the closest thing he ever got to a real home after having left Odense, but it was still complicated, for he remained a working-class lad deep down. At one point in his portrait of his life in *The Fairy Tale of My Life* (*Mit Livs Eventyr*, 1855), Andersen refers to himself as a "swamp plant" that has roots deep down in the mud, but that stretches upwards after the light and finally reaches the surface where he can unfold his leaves in the wonderful sunshine.

It was virtually impossible to break through the fixed social and cultural patterns that existed in the first half of the 19th century, where people lived in social classes and ordered in a carefully determined hierarchy. Hans Christian was nevertheless successful in doing so. He became a social and cultural mould-breaker. He left the duck-yard!

Practically all his writing dealt with that theme: the ugly duckling that had lain in a swan's egg! It grew beautiful, but was given a hard time of it in the process. But he also wrote in his tales about the shadows and the pain that eternally follow the individual who breaks free of the known in order to conquer the unknown. That pain and loneliness incessantly beset Andersen, who, even when had become famous, admitted that he was working-class deep down.

Hans Christian made his literary debut in 1829 with the humorous *Fodreise fra Holmens Canal til Østpynten af Amager i Aarene 1828-29* (Journey on Foot from Holmen's Canal to the Eastern Point of Amager in the Years 1828 and 1829). His first poems were also published in 1829. He wrote plays, novels, librettos for operas, and travel books. He quickly became recognized, among other things for his first novel, *Improvisatoren* (*The Improvisatore*), which was published in 1835. That same year, *Eventyr, fortalte for Børn. Første Samling. Første Hefte* (Tales Told for Children. Book One) was also published. With them he once again broke the mould with tales that made world literature. A new literary universe opened with these fairy tales and stories. The first of them appeared as a booklet with a total of four, then later seven tales. Andersen himself regarded the fairy tales as stories that were for children, but told by an adult – so they were for all ages. They are for the childlike, for fantasy, and for children of all ages. For life!

The Artist's Restless Desire for Change

From around 1840 onwards, Hans Christian Andersen's star rose high in the sky. He became known in Germany in the 1840s and that led to a strengthening of his reputation and fame in Denmark as well as in Europe, not long after in USA, and Russia, and later again – after his death – in Asia (Ye Rulan, "HCA in China"). In his own lifetime, he saw his fame unfold and he became recognized. But he never *felt properly* recognized in his soul and true identity. He went on feeling "wrong" and constantly experienced the pain involved in being a mould-breaker who deep down knew he was a child of the working-class. He was insatiable when it came to praise. He basked in praise like Narcissus at his own reflection, desiring recognition but incapable of daring to believe in it.

Andersen never was at peace with himself, never established a home, but travelled a great deal and wrote constantly while on his journeys.

What he saw he turned into experiences via this eternal writing in diaries, letters, and fiction. He became a cosmopolitan who visited practically all the countries in Europe. His travels also took him to social functions with dukes, barons, kings, and celebrities of the time. He visited such famous figures and scientists as Victor Hugo, Charles Dickens, the Brothers Grimm and J.C.P. von Schelling. In Denmark he did a grand tour of the great manor houses, where he stayed for long periods of time. Andersen liked to picture himself as someone from one of his favourite childhood fairy tales, *Aladdin*, who gets the orange in his turban and happiness as a gift of grace, because he possesses an inner fantasy and destiny. It was not easy for Andersen, who was no Aladdin. He had to work extremely hard to become a writer and, in a sense, give up his life for his writing.

Hans Christian Andersen himself presented his life as one long fairy tale with obstacles that were overcome but also with happiness that could never be kept hold of. It was the total life-story that he himself formed in *The Fairy Tale of My Life* from 1855, which begins with the words, "My life is a lovely fairy tale, so rich and blessed." (My translation). Here the writer organises his life and his posthumous reputation in the form of a fairy tale. He gives his life to the fairy tale, one could say, he turns his life into literature and thereby sacrifices himself for his art. In that sense, he renounced his own life and shifted the question of happiness and existence into the inner space of art.

Hans Christian Andersen *the man* was wildly in love with women on several occasions in his life, but he never realized a love-relationship, partly perhaps because he lacked the social competencies required to approach a girl in that manner. Partly too, because he let *the writer* Hans Christian Andersen use the feeling of love as material in his fairy tales. He fell in love several times, as mentioned. The first time it was in the beautiful Riborg Voigt, who, however, became engaged to another man. Later he fell in love with the singer Jenny Lind, the Swedish "Nightingale", who did not want to have him, but offered to "be as a sister" for him. Erotic love was something the writer probably never experienced. He had to live *his* life, observing and describing life. Andersen gradually assumed the role of the writer and adapted himself to it. Life was in art and literature, while the writer himself was outside as the one whose task it was to observe and depict life, but without being able to participate in it.

The Chinese Fairy Tale

In *The Fairy Tale of My Life* Andersen relates a dream he had as a child. He had moved with his parents to a street near Munkemølle Port (the city gate), and used to play down by the river, singing away at the top of his voice and often with people listening from the next-door garden:

> When they had company in the garden they were always listening to my singing, and I knew it. All told me that I had a beautiful voice, which would bring me luck in the world. I often meditated how this luck should come, and as the wonderful has always been truth for me, so I expected the most marvellous things would happen.
>
> An old woman who rinsed clothes in the river, told me that the Empire of China was situated straight under the very river of Odense, and I did not find it impossible at all that a Chinese prince, some moonlight night when I was sitting there, might dig himself through the earth up to us, hear me sing, and so take me down with him to his kingdom, make me rich and noble, and then let me again visit Odense, where I would live and build me a castle. (17, 29)[2]

It is strange that Andersen dreamt Chinese dreams like that. In the story that he himself called "My Chinese Fairy Tale", namely "The Nightingale" from 1843, it says:

> The Emperor of China is a Chinaman, as you most likely know, and everyone around him is a Chinaman too. It's been a great many years since this story happened in China, but that's all the more reason for telling it before it gets forgotten. (1, 271)

There is the mentioned memory of a Chinese prince in a dream that occurs here, but otherwise things are quite Chinese in China, one understands:

> The Emperor's palace was the wonder of the world. It was made entirely of fine porcelain, extremely expensive but so delicate that you could touch it only with the greatest of care. In the garden the rarest flowers bloomed,

---

2 The English translation is from *The Fairy Tale of My Life*, p. 19.

and to the prettiest ones were tied little silver bells which tinkled so that no one could pass by without noticing them. Yes, all things were arranged according to plan in the Emperor's garden, though how far and wide it extended not even the gardener knew. (1, 271)

It is a fairytale country that would be well worth visiting, so odd and 'contrived', so vast and fine as it clearly is. It is, as Jacob Bøggild has drawn attention to in his thesis (*Svævende stasis*), a fantastic word-play Andersen is indulging in here, for he is also playing on a secondary meaning of the word *kinesisk* that was quite common at the time we often refer to as The Golden Age, i.e. that of Hans Christian Andersen, when the word for "Chinese" could refer to that which "maintains antiquated, troublesome or long-winded traditions". The adjective could also mean "awkward and complicated". (*Svævende stasis* 99). In English, the word for good-quality porcelain is in fact "china", so there are so many Chinese associations that I hardly need mention that an orange got its Danish name *appelsin* at the same period, via *Apfel sino*', i.e. Chinese apple. Well, well! The joke and the play on words become quite sublime in "The Shepherdess and the Chimney Sweep" ("Hyrdinden og Skorsteensfeieren", 1845) where,

> Near them stood another figure, three times as big as they were. It was an old Chinaman who could nod his head. He too was made of porcelain, and he said he was the little shepherdess's grandfather. But he couldn't prove it. Nevertheless he claimed that this gave him authority over her, and when General-Headquarters-Hindquarters-Gives-Orders-Front-and-Rear-Sergeant-Billygoat-Legs asked for her hand in marriage, the old Chinaman had nodded consent. (1, 357-358)

Now that we know how Andersen in this small object pantomime of a fairy tale, as elsewhere, plays on the fact that *chinese* and *kinesisk* at that time can mean both porcelain and something that is old and stiff, the floodgates open for Andersen's narrative art. We recall how things turn out for the old Chinaman in the fairy tale here, for he falls off the shelf and breaks his stiff, Chinese porcelain neck:

> The chimney-sweep and the little shepherdess looked so pleadingly at the old Chinaman, for they were deathly afraid he would nod. But he didn't.

He couldn't. And neither did he care to tell anyone that, forever and a day, he'd have to wear a rivet in his neck.

So the little porcelain people remained together. They thanked goodness for the rivet in grandfather's neck, and they kept on loving each other until the day they broke. (1, 361)

Here Andersen demonstrates his virtuosity as a storyteller, the way in which he can create a quite distinctive richness of images. China and the idea of the Chinese play a role in 19th century Europe, including Denmark, as the kingdom that was so strange and so odd and magical that there was no end to it. It lay on the far side of the globe and by many Europeans it was considered to be a fairytale kingdom which, in many ways, was a complete contrast to Europe. The kingdom lay at the end of the Silk Road, which was a famous route to the mysterious Orient and to things and objects, spices, silks etc. that were thought of in Europe as fairy tale and exotic to the highest degree.

There are not many children after Hans Christian Andersen who have not dreamt of digging a hole so deep that one came down to the Chinese. That is what Andersen is playing on in his fairy tale about the little nightingale. And a nightingale is not just any sort of bird for Andersen. As a boy he was sometimes referred to as "Odense's Nightingale" because he went round singing with his high, fine soprano voice. It was that voice which he believed would lead to him becoming famous when, as a 14-year-old boy, he set off for Copenhagen. Unfortunately, however, the nightingale's voice broke and he then sounded like a crow!

Then, in 1843, a new nightingale starts to sing. It is the 23-year-old Swedish singer Jenny Lind, who is visiting Copenhagen. She was known as "the Swedish Nightingale" for her fantastic voice, and all of Copenhagen idolised her. Andersen met her at the home of the director of The Royal Ballet in Copenhagen, August Bournonville, himself an admirer of Jenny Lind. The meeting with her set Andersen ablaze with a fire so strong and violent that he could hardly bear it. The Swedish nightingale created poetry and trilling in his soul which, among other things, he transmuted into the fairy tale "The Nightingale", where the former childhood dream of the Chinese prince and his infatuation with "the Swedish Nightingale" merged to form a story that depicts art and love as the only true things in this world. He never won "his" Jenny Nightingale. Nor did he win Riborg Voigt. He was incapable of realizing love in the erotic sense. But he was wonderfully capable of transforming great emotions into the nightingale's song of art.

Hans Christian Andersen, then, repeatedly tells us the highly modern story of being a restless, seeking mould-breaker, of desiring recognition and not wanting to remain in one's present position. A story and an emotion many modern people can see themselves in. Indeed, it is perhaps not at all possible today to refrain from mirroring oneself in all this, for it is a part of modern life and its conditions.

To Seek Oneself

Hans Christian Andersen was forced to shift his longings for love over into the fairy tales he wrote. And in general he was, as mentioned, a person and an artist who constantly broke new ground in his art because he was never able to rest in the outer reality he encountered. He travelled round Europe many times, something that is reflected in his fairy tales and stories, which are a rich treasure trove of locations and experiences. He visited kings, dukes, scientists and artists, places and landscapes throughout his life, because he was full of an unquenchable thirst for experiences and a restless searching for the inner balance he only found in his art, but never in his life. All of Europe as well as a colossal panorama of the world is present in his works, which include fantastic travel books and sensitively portrayed moods and atmospheres. His first novel, *The Improvisatore*, is an autobiographical portrayal of an artist who cannot refrain from improvising and creating art, because he finds art more real than lived life.

Hans Christian Andersen develops in his work so many themes that, paradoxically, contain in many ways themes and traits that can seem more characteristic of modern individuals here at the beginning of the 21st century than they actually were for people in the 19th century. In his art, Andersen was:

- a social and cultural mould-breaker
- a restless traveller
- a soul, seeking identity
- a self-staging narcissist
- a man hungering for recognition without ever being able to find full satisfaction in it

Andersen's art does not only include much that today can be read and perceived as highly modern. He was modern in his own age in the sense that he loved and praised modern technology and its potential. He loved the power of the steam engine and the railways, which he saw being laid down like long tracks of dreams through Europe. He predicted in his travel book *I Sverrig* (*In Sweden*) from 1851 how people some day would come to fly, and how speed would become like electric shocks through the body. He even, in "The Galoshes of Fortune" ("Lykkens Kalosker", 1838), predicted what it must be like to walk on the moon, namely "to walk in newly fallen snow." That is a prediction about the surface of the moon that the American astronaut Buzz Aldrin confirmed in 1969 when he walked on the moon as the second man, after Armstrong. Andersen travelled to the World Exposition in Paris in 1867 and was enthusiastic about machines, light and the modern city. In the fairy tale "The Dryad" ("Dryaden", 1868), he lets the small tree-spirit long to leave the security of its tree to seek the light, the mobility and freedom of the modern world. One of the people he admired most was the physicist Hans Christian Ørsted, who described electromagnetism, and through long conversations with him, Andersen saw the modern technological possibilities as a true fairy tale. Andersen even allowed the fish on the sea-bed to discuss the "new cousin" in the shape of the large sea-serpent in the fairy tale "The Great Sea-Serpent" ("Den store Søslange", 1872) which depicts a fish's-eye view of one of the world's new technological wonders – the telegraph cable between Europe and USA, which was laid down on the bed of the Atlantic Ocean in the 1860s.

In his art, Andersen linked the tradition and the modern in his stories and fairy tales, just as he created an artistic link between the near and the distant. Neither are his artistic work, fantasy, and depiction of human emotions limited to a Danish or European context. Nor are his narrative powers confined to the century in which he lived and wrote, but to all ages where people live and dream. Hans Christian Andersen is the great writer of human emotions who addresses children, and adults, the child in the adult and that which is of value and worth in both children and adults. He is a great narrator in China, and in Denmark, and in the world. And it is fantastic that he creates a link between Danish and Chinese culture through the hole in the earth beneath the river that stretches from a Danish teller of fairy tales to millions of people in the most populous country in the world.

The Reception of Hans Christian Andersen on Campus

Sun Jian
Professor, Director of the Nordic Literature Research Institute,
Fudan University

The workshop[1] sponsored jointly by the University of Southern Denmark and Fudan University on the topic of *The Cultural and National Significance of Hans Christian Andersen in China and Denmark* was a continuation of our scholarly collaboration which started at Fudan University in November 2011 where a similar seminar was held to explore how the fairy tales of Hans Christian Andersen crossed the cultural boundaries and gained acceptance in China. Professor Johs. Frandsen, Professor Torben G. Jeppesen and I, together with our colleagues at the two universities have been encouraged by the academic achievement and are determined to further promote this collegiate exchange. As a scholar of Nordic literature and a teacher, I will focus in my paper on the reception of Hans Christian Andersen on campus at Fudan University.

It is known to all, Hans Christian Andersen enjoyed a great popularity in China when his works, especially his fairy tales, were first translated into Chinese at the beginning of the 20th century, at a time when China was undergoing great changes both socially and politically. Together with other translated literary works from the West, Hans Christian Andersen's fairy tales played an important role in the process of the Chinese modernization. To varying degrees, Hans Christian Andersen was connected to the schools and universities and became one of the great inspirers for the students and intellectuals who pioneered in the New Culture Movement and the May Fourth movement,[2] a cultural renaissance which aimed at breaking up the feudal system in China

---

1 I refer to the workshop held at the University of Southern Denmark in Odense in October, 2012.
2 The May Fourth Movement took place in Peking on 4 May, 1919, and the New Culture Movement also started at that time.

and freeing people physically and spiritually from the old ideas and manners. Hu Shi,[3] one of the pioneers, highlights the essence of the New Culture Movement in a penetrating paper entitled "The Chinese Renaissance":

> First, it was a conscious movement to promote a new literature in the living language of the people to take the place of the classical literature of old. Second, it was a movement of conscious protest against many of the ideas and institutions in the traditional culture, and of conscious emancipation of the individual man and woman from the bondage of the forces of tradition. (Hu Shi 79)

In a sense, the fairy tales of Hans Christian Andersen, for many progressive intellectuals in China at that time, represented new ideas from the West and they also provided a novel form of literature for children and young people and, furthermore, they helped to enlighten those Chinese people who were eager to embrace a modernized China. Heinrich Detering is right to point out the suitability of Andersen's writings for the new age, "Seen as a whole, they (his writings) form one large strenuous attempt to find a poetry for the new age he lived in, without giving up the traditions he himself was raised in and which were so dear to him." (64).

For some reason, Hans Christian Andersen was not overtly presented at universities in China after the liberation in 1949. He was a favourite subject in kindergartens, primary schools and high schools, where some of his fairy tales were included in textbooks. He was mentioned only in courses like Western literature and the history of world literature at universities and the descriptions of his tales were very general and sometimes politically biased. This situation remained unchanged until 2005, when a Nordic literature course was initiated at Fudan University with Hans Christian Andersen as the first of the

---

3   Hu Shi 胡适 (1891-1962) was born in Shanghai. Later he obtained a scholarship and studied agriculture at Cornell University in America. In 1912, he changed his major to philosophy and literature. He later got a position teaching philosophy at Peking University, where he collaborated with Chen Duxiu, editor of the influential journal *New Youth* and quickly gained much attention and started to popularize his radical ideas in the journal, which was extremely popular among the students and teachers. Hu contributed greatly to the Chinese social, cultural and language reform. He made great efforts in introducing vernacular Chinese (bai hua) during the New Culture Movement and later the May Fourth Movement as one of the acknowledged leading figures.

three authors on the syllabus. The course, which was the first on the Nordic classics in Chinese universities, has proved to be very successful since its inauguration. It has attracted the attention of students from different disciplines at Fudan.

The setting up of the course was largely a result of the establishment of the Nordic Center at Fudan and the subsequent inauguration of the Nordic Literary Research Institute, which aims at bringing Nordic classics into close contact with students who want to learn more about Nordic literature and explore Hans Christian Andersen's fairy tales further. And the teaching of his fairy tales is in accordance with the overall strategy of the university in an effort to expose the students to more canonical writings, to inculcate humanistic ideas into their heads and to promote cross-culture exchanges. Under the auspices of the institute and with the endeavour on the part of the hard-working teachers, more and more students have developed interests in Nordic literature. And the influx of many internationally renowned scholars and professors from the Nordic universities has enabled the students to enlarge their academic horizon by attending the lectures and speeches given by the visitors. At the same time, high level academic exchanges run parallel with those classes and lectures – and the workshop that we have successfully conducted is a case in point.

The revival of interest in Andersen's fairy tales on campus also manifests the quickening pace of the process of globalization, as more and more people, students in particular, realize that it is important to get to know different cultures in order to prepare themselves adequately for the future and for the greater modernity that started in China a century ago. When commenting on the idea of globalization, Fredric Jameson says, "Clearly enough, the concept of globalization reflects the sense of an immense enlargement of world communication, as well as of the horizon of a world market, both of which seem far more tangible and immediate than in earlier stages of modernity" (Jameson xi).

For decades, the students at Fudan have been exposed mostly to English and American literature, which dominates the university syllabus. Those courses have been taught and exhausted by endless analysis and repetitions. The students want to have something new, something that can offer a vital alternative, reveal new truths and give them new perspectives. With the Nordic literature course, the students can gain access to an alternative literature besides the English and American ones. And Hans Christian Andersen's fairy tales, I venture to argue, offer them a new perspective which is vital, challenging and topical. The diversity of the subject matters in those literary courses does indeed provide opportunities for the students to come into contact with not only one "other" but many "others". Gabriele Schwab, when talking about the transitional space of literature, says, "The notion of a transitional space of literature emphasizes not only the affinities but also the difference between reading and other forms of cultural contact. (...) Therefore we may, in the transitional space, act out fantasies and fears, enact relations that would otherwise be restricted if not taboo, or temporarily dissolve boundaries that are necessary to maintain in actual cultural encounters. We may expose ourselves to a dissolution of the boundaries between the real and the imaginary, which would otherwise induce a psychotic experience." (Schwab 26).

The enthusiasm and interest the students have displayed in his works are greater than I had expected. The forty to fifty students in a class I usually work with are those whom we in China call kids born in the 1980s and 1990s. They are sometimes regarded negatively as spoilt kids, nicknamed "little emperors and empresses". However, they belong to a unique group that is dynamic, critical and sometimes very radical. They view the world very differently from the youth who rose up in the May Fourth Movement and from their parents, born after the liberation and during the Cultural Revolution. Brought up in the hectic years of opening up, reform and fast economic development, they have witnessed the drastic changes in Chinese economy and society.

Most of the students are familiar with some of the popular fairy tales by Hans Christian Andersen. As children, they often had Andersen's tales read to them as bedtime stories. When the parents read the tales, they often added and deleted things as they wished, making their listeners passive receivers of the adapted truth. When the children entered primary schools and high schools, they got to know some selected readings of Hans Christian Andersen's stories without the possibility of getting a comprehensive understanding of the writer's whole attitude to life and his aesthetic principles.

To improve the situation, we not only focus on the most popular fairy tales of Hans Christian Andersen in class, such as "The Ugly Duckling", "The Little Mermaid", "The Snow Queen", "The Match Girl", "The Red Shoes", "The Emperor's New Clothes", "The Nightingale", and so on, but we also discuss the more difficult ones such as "The Shadow" and encourage the students to read more by giving them a reading list.

As the students are grown-ups and their views about life are getting more mature and sophisticated, we encourage them to dig deeper into Hans Christian Andersen's fairy tales and use their imagination in reading the texts. This really involves a change of roles, since now they are no longer passive receivers but active thinkers. They read instead of being read to. Moreover, class discussions, seminars and activities related to Andersen enable the students to understand the multivalent nature of his works and to rediscover the artistic value of the fairy tales. Needless to say, the students have benefited a lot in the process of reconstructing Hans Christian Andersen's fairy tales. The following examples from the term papers well illustrate the ideas and critical thinking of the students.

In a paper entitled "Surviving or Thriving", one girl student from the Department of Psychology[4] wrote: "I read this title a few years ago in a report on kids with studying disabilities. When reading 'The Ugly Duckling' again in this course, this title pumped into my mind. Through the feelings of the ugly duckling, we can get a deeper understanding of the story and obtain enlightenment for our life."

Chen Hao from the Department of Mechanics and Engineering Science says in his paper "My Simple Opinions on Andersen's 'The Ugly Duckling,' I think are very humble, weak and small. As I am standing in front of God, my weakness in thought, speech and behaviour expand. I feel like Andersen on the day when he was awarded 'Honourable Citizen of Odense'. We should fight with faith and strive to achieve our dreams just like the ugly duckling."

Huang Huifang, majoring in Chinese, says in his paper "Pseudo Hideousness": "Nevertheless, what is most intriguing about the ugly duckling is that he followed his heart of doing what he most wanted to (swimming in the water) and he dared to step out of his comfort zone in pursuit of his own dreams. He took the risk to be different, to be himself even in the face of death. I think it is this passion and courage of living his way of life that made him superior to the others."

Jiang Yuxin, another student from the Chinese Department, offers his afterthought upon finishing reading "The Ugly Duckling": "We can't depend on luck for a living and most of us are still ugly ducklings. All

---

[4] My students have kindly given me permission to quote freely from their papers.

we can do is to adapt ourselves to this ugly world. Pain makes you stronger, tears make you braver and fairy tales make us know better."

In their papers, they have all shown their excitement after rereading Andersen's fairy tales and the rediscovery of the charm of the tales has given them much aesthetic experience. And they share the idea of the translator Eric Christian Haugaard, whose English version is used as textbook by the students, "Andersen lived seventy years; and I believe his fairy tales will live forever. (...) The fairy tale speaks to all of us; that is its particular charm." (Haugaard xiii).

Among the fairy tales of Hans Christian Andersen, "The Little Mermaid" remains the students' favourite. For one thing, the tale has one moving storyline, then, Andersen offers readers a unique perspective, and what is more, the bronze statue of the Little Mermaid created by Danish Sculptor Edvard Eriksen travelled thousands of miles all the way from the harbour in Copenhagen to the Shanghai Expo held in 2010 and stayed in the Danish Pavilion for six months, the first long journey she had taken since she was unveiled in 1913. The "journey" of the statue aroused a great controversy in Denmark. But the idea of travelling is all the more significant. Hans Christian Andersen, according to Professor Sven Hakon Rossel, "was one of the greatest travellers" (Rossel 1) and he lived for travelling.

> To travel, however, also meant for the artist Andersen to find motifs and themes abroad which could later be used in his writing. Not only did his travel activities and experiences in general find their immediate expression in his travelogues, but also the individual experiences, episodes, and the visual sensations and sensory impressions were employed everywhere in his work. (Rossel 3)

Li Zhenghuan, majoring in business management, wrote in his paper entitled "The Significance of the Marble Statue in Andersen's 'The Little Mermaid'": "The little mermaid had a white and beautiful marble statue of a human body before meeting the prince. And the marble statue stands for the desire of the little mermaid. The little mermaid loves the human prince. However what she really desires for is the eternal soul. The colors white and red separately stand for different significance."

Ye Xuanyu, a student majoring in philosophy, also focuses on the marble statue in "The Little Mermaid" by referring to the metaphorical meaning of the object: "Through the little mermaid's journey, we have carefully analysed all the metaphorical implications of the marble statue: the love for the prince, the silence, and the suppression of emotion. It is really surprising to find that a tiny object in an inconspicuous paragraph can represent so many important themes of the story and help connect them in this tale."

One student of the business management major is clearly bewitched by the little mermaid and her love toward the prince and he wrote: "The story of the little mermaid ends in a tragedy but I want to passionately fall in love with someone like the little mermaid before I die. To me, her love is very beautiful and so worthy. She has her own values and opinion at least but I have not stuck to my acting and thinking."

Hu Jialin, a girl majoring in economics, tries to make a distinction between love and agape: "Agape is not love. Love between a man and a woman is selfish, excluded while agape is unconditional, selfless, just like the way Jesus Christ loves human beings. Now we see that the little mermaid is actually a religious story; it tells about religion, redemption and agape instead of love."

Tang Jingyi, majoring in Nuclear Science and Technology, points to the Faust dilemma in "The Little Mermaid", claiming that "The prince had become one symbol of her desire for a long time. We all remember the little gardens each princess had and the little mermaid's was filled with sun-like plants and a statue of a boy. The statue is an immortal work to some extent and it fits her desire well. The gardens all present their owners' favourites, but only the youngest mermaid had a clear desire. The Mephisto had been with her from her childhood because Mephisto was her desire."

Gong Miaoxin, a girl from the Department of Nuclear Science and Technology, made a comparative study of "The Snow Queen" and "The Ice Maiden" by touching upon the existential problems. "The ending of 'The Snow Queen' is in a sense flawed as well. It abides by the logic of the tale and the unity of its universe. The universe of 'The Ice Maiden', however, does not possess any unity. It is fundamentally split, and its parts seem to contradict each other. The conversion is that Andersen does not trust the force of his own story and he directly intervenes to set things straight, leaving an ending which seems 'half chopped off' on 'The Snow Queen' and another which seems realistic on 'The Ice Maiden'."

When explaining why she picked up "The Match Girl" as her favourite, one Swedish girl taking the course concluded after a lengthy analysis: "So to sum up the above said, 'The Little Match Girl' is one of my favourite fairy tales because of its magic aura surrounding it and its portrayal of a difficult part of life-death. It is beautifully written and it should be told again and again to Children of future generations so that everyone has a chance of taking part in Andersen's magical and enchanted world of fairy tales."

Most of the students have experienced growing pains and may face a tougher life and even an existential dilemma after graduation. They have really gained from Andersen's fairy tales in terms of enlightenment, inspiration and courage. As Bruno Bettelheim puts it: "It is characteristic of fairy tales to state an existential dilemma briefly and pointedly. This permits the child to come to grips with the problem in its most essential form, where a more complex plot would confuse matters for him." (Bettelheim 9).

In their papers, many students compared Andersen's tales with their own life stories. Commenting on Andersen's love, a girl student has this to say: "There are different kinds of love, but they are all love. In my childhood, my favourite fairy tales of Andersen were 'The Little Mermaid' and 'What Father Does Is Always Right', although actually these two are different as far as styles are concerned. Maybe the reason why I liked them was that they have the same essence – love." She then concluded: "Andersen impressed me as being both very fastidious and self-abased. These two words seem contradictory, but the contradiction is Andersen's distinct feature. He wanted perfect love, but his self-abased characteristic blocked his way. His fantasy did not come true. It's very tragic for him, but it is fortunate for literature."

In their critiques of Andersen, they are very straightforward in their comments and arguments, relating his tales to the problems of a fast-changing society and expressing their concerns about the bad effect brought about by the worshipping of material gains and the breaking-up of family relationships. Besides regarding Hans Christian Andersen as a social critic, many students concentrated on the love he showed for people, old and young, animals, and even vegetations. Inspired by his tales, some students have explored deeper and tried to interpret the stories in philosophical and even psychological terms. Many examples can be cited to show the literary sensitivity and the dynamo of those young people and in a word, university is a place where all kinds of thoughts and ideas meet and respond nakedly to each other. Whatever changes take place, humanism is always at the core of all disciplines. And it is our mission, as professors and scholars of literature to expose students to the great works of the masters and to stand our ground with confidence in human virtues and values.

> Humanity! Can you understand the bliss of such a moment, when your spirit, your art, knows its mission? The moment when all the pain endured along the thorny path – even that self-inflicted – becomes knowledge, truth, power, clearness, and health? The disharmony becomes harmony, and this revelation that God grants one man, he, in turn, gives to all humanity. (Andersen, *Complete Fairy Tales* 486)

In a word, Hans Christian Andersen is just like this man who serves as a bridge between man and God and his tales are like "The story of the thorny path" which "does not end as a fairy tale in bliss and happiness here on earth, it reaches out into space and into eternity." (Andersen, *Complete Fairy Tales* 486).[5]

---

5 See "The Thorny Path" by Hans Christian Andersen.

Ransoming Andersen
China's Reception of Hans Christian Andersen and the Dilemma of its Andersen Studies

Lu Li'an
Professor, Research Fellow of the Nordic Literature
Research Institute, Fudan University

This essay[1] is a critical genealogical study of the Chinese reception of the work of Hans Christian Andersen, with a dual focus on the specific socio-political agenda that shaped the mode of introduction then and its lasting impact on children's literature in China today. The key contention is that the popularization of Andersen's fairy tales in early 20th century China was synchronous with China's modernizing movements such as the New Culture Movement and the rise of Socialism, which, to some extent, effects a consistent politicized understanding of Andersen's major fairy tales. To investigate how contemporary China receives Andersen, this paper studies various present-day academic and scholarly critiques of "The Little Mermaid", leading to a discussion of current dilemmas as well as future prospects regarding Andersen studies in China.

I. Translation is a Creative Force in Modern Chinese Literature: How Andersen Studies in China Came to Be

Translation can be a creative force in literature, Cay Dollerup argues convincingly in his study of the birth of the European bourgeois fairy tale: "begun as but a 'small' genre, literary fairy tale soon grew to become 'international' owing to the efforts of literati who served not only as translators but also practitioners" (94-102). Dollerup's point more

---

[1] I would like to thank the generous funding of Fudan University 985 Key-Project (2011RWXKZD026) which sponsored various inspiring academic communications with Andersen scholars from the University of Southern Denmark. I also want to thank Shanghai Pujiang Program (KBH3152525) for facilitating part of the research and the completion of this paper.

than cogently applies to the scale of creative influence of Hans Christian Andersen on China's modern literary landscape – to the extent that China's children's literature has categorically held Hans Christian Andersen to be its progenitor. Andersen's fame soared as soon as he was introduced to the early 20th century Chinese literati. Subsequently, translations of his tales appeared, giving rise to further commentaries. From the 1910s to the 1960s, such responses were largely published in literary magazines, gazettes, or as Translators' Forewords prefacing collections of Andersen's fairy tales. If we review the process of canonization of Andersen in China, it is not difficult to detect how the reception of this writer was deeply intertwined with China's project of enlightenment and modernization, which manifests itself in various dimensions such as nation-building, nationhood formation, and the institutionalization of knowledge production.

The first Chinese biography of Andersen is *The Fairy Tale Writer Andersen* (《童话作家安徒生》; 1955) written by Ye Junjian (叶君健), which is based on Andersen's own autobiographical accounts. During the Cultural Revolution decade (1966-1977) all research on foreign literature was virtually halted; when it was resumed, academic interests started to emerge to enrich the existent promotional, popularizing studies of Andersen, though he was mostly studied in relation to China's children's literature. The first academic monograph within Andersen Studies in China was published in 1984, titled *A Brief Study of Hans Christian Andersen* (《安徒生简论》), by Pu Manting (浦漫汀), (Wang Quangen, *Andersen Research* 6).[2]

Since 2000, Andersen Studies in China has gathered momentum and produced three indispensable monographs to document this Dane's influence in China. Marking the bicentennial of Andersen's birth and celebrating the centennial of his introduction into China, 2005 saw the publication of Wang Quangen's *Andersen Research in China For One Hundred Years* (王泉根,《中国安徒生研究一百年》) and Li Hongye's *Chinese Interpretations of Andersen's Fairy Tales* (李红叶,《安徒生童话的中国阐释》).

Wang Quangen's book assembles major Chinese commentaries of Andersen's fairy tales from the late 1910s to 2003, among which some

---

[2] Pu Manting, professor of Chinese Literature at Beijing Normal University. Pu's achievement laid the foundation for studying Andersen's fairy tales in relation to the discipline of children's literature.

are grouped together as "Classical Interpretation". Similarly, Li Hongye's book explores the response of three major Chinese translators of Andersen[3] and traces Chinese reception of Andersen's fairy tales as children's literature in the second half of the 20th century. The year 2009 saw the publication of *Andersen's Fairy Tales and China's Modern Children's Literature*, by Wang Lei (王蕾,《安徒生童话与中国现代儿童文学》). Wang's work draws heavily on Li's and Wang's research to explain Andersen's influence on major Chinese writers of children's literature. These three monographs, now staple resources for Chinese scholars within Andersen Studies, all attempt to relate the rise of China's children's literature to Andersen's translated tales in China. Yet, in my view, a more fruitful understanding of Andersen Studies in China can be achieved if we do it the other way round – by placing the translation/interpretation history of Andersen's fairy tales into the historical context of 20th century China. I argue – with all due respect to both Hans Christian Andersen and China's children's literature – that Andersen's unshakable eminence in China as *the* children's writer fails to do him justice. In fact, it is somewhat self-limiting for Andersen studies in China, because the author wrote for both children and grown-ups; besides, he was a versatile writer of short stories, dramas, and poems, and recent scholarly focus has shown him to be a talented artist in paper cutting, sketching, and paper-collage as well. To read Hans Christian Andersen as *only* a fairy tale writer for children is a dated, narrow perspective.

To begin with my inquiry: When and how did China first learn of the name of Hans Christian Andersen? Which of his tales was translated first?

A consensus holds that Andersen was introduced to China by the joint efforts of Zhou Zuoren[4] and his elder brother Zhou Shuren, *aka* Lu Xun[5]. However, exactly *when* that happened is less easy to ascertain. As early as in 1909, in order to promote further subscription and sales of their literary journal, Zhou and Lu Xun mentioned in their *Collection*

---

3   These three major translators of Andersen's tales in the first half of the 20th century China are Zhou Zuoren (周作人), Zheng Zhenduo (郑振铎), and Zhao Jingshen (赵景深).
4   Zhou Zuoren, 周作人, 1885-1967, anthropologist, essayist, literary scholar, folklorist, theorist of children's literature, and poet.
5   Zhou Shuren, 周树人, 1881-1936, known as Lu Xun (鲁迅), eminent literary scholar, writer, thinker, critic, and revolutionary.

of *Foreign Novels, Vol. II* (《域外小说集》第二集) that the next issue would include a story by Andersen; unfortunately, however, volume III never appeared (Wang Lei 56-57; Li Hongye, *Chinese Interpretations* 14). If this mention is too brief to count, 1912 certainly is often taken as the year when Andersen's name officially became known in China, as Zhou Zuoren in an essay on the short-story genre briefly mentioned him (Li Hongye, *Chinese Interpretations* 13; Wu Qinan 127). Nonetheless, other scholars hold that it is 1913 when Andersen was properly introduced into China, as that is when a full account of Andersen's life and work, written by Zhou and titled "The Danish Poet Andersen", appeared (Li Hongye, *Chinese Interpretations* 9-14; Wang Quangen, *Andersen Research* 3). It should be noted that Andersen, in Zhou's two introductions, was never referred to as a "writer of fairy tales" (Wang Quangen, *Andersen Research* 1-5).[6]

However, in spite of such general consensus about Zhou Zuoren "bringing" Andersen to China, disagreement nonetheless exists. Li Hongye gives Sun Yuxiu as the introducer of Andersen in the China of 1908 (*Chinese Interpretations* 27).[7] Wang Lei partly agrees with this view but she differs in pointing to 1909 as the year when Sun first introduced Andersen within the context of European and American novelists; but whatever the year, in Sun's introductions, Andersen was a supernatural fantasist, a writer of wonder tales, not a writer of fairy tales *per se* (58-61).

The first story by Andersen introduced to China in 1914 is "The Emperor's New Clothes", translated by the notable linguist and writer Liu Bannong (刘半农). However, what Liu did to this tale was hardly translation but *transcription* – he took the liberty of deleting passages and rewriting the story, barely retaining the basic gist (Wang Quangen, *Andersen Research* 3; Li Hongye, *Chinese Interpretations* 14; Wang Lei 61-62).

In 1917, Andersen's "The Old Tombstone" was translated by Zhou Shoujuan (周瘦鹃) and included in the *Collection of Famous European*

---

[6] Drawn indirectly from essays by Edmund Gosse and George Boyesen, Zhou mistook the city of Odense as the island of Funen, and spent much space deliberating Andersen's appearances and life stories, praising his child-like – and childish – writing features, such as personification. Zhou's remark is quoted in Wang Quangen, *Andersen Research* 1-5.

[7] Sun Yuxiu, 孙毓修, 1871-1922, scholar and editor of children's literature of early republican China. Sun would spend the following 15 years translating "The Steadfast Tin Solider" and "The Little Mermaid" for the series of *Literature for Children* (《童话》) that he edited (Li Hongye, *Chinese Interpretations* 27).

and American Short Stories along with a short bio and a picture of Andersen. Both Sun's and Zhou's introductions align Andersen's tales with the genre of the supernatural, folkloric, and fantastical stories with which Chinese readers were fairly familiar. Therefore, Andersen, during the first decade of his entry into China (1908-1917), was seen largely as a spinner of wonder tales, not a writer of fairy tales, let alone a writer for children. His representative tales included "The Ugly Duckling", "The Snow Queen", "The Little Mermaid", etc. But, what must be pointed out is: common literary practice of the early 20th century China continued to use the classical/literary Chinese (文言文) as the medium of writing and publication. In nature, classical Chinese is highly condensed and compact and approximates more to verse than to prose. The introduction of foreign writers and works was then often rendered, not in faithful translation, but in paraphrasing summary. And as one would expect all Andersen-translation and/or commentary, like most early 20th century Chinese publication, were read not by the common folk but by the educated elite. It would take the New Culture Movement (1915-1919) and its culmination, the May Fourth Movement (1919), to revamp Andersen as a writer of fairy tales – a writer exclusively for children.

II. Andersen and Chinese Literature for Children: Rediscovering Children for the Nation

In view of China's feebleness, political reformers since the late Qing Dynasty had argued for a wholesale reform of education.[8] This momentum to westernize also spurred the translation boom of Western literature out of which arose a cultural and literary category: Children's Literature.[9] The rise of China's children's literature was closely related to its project of modernization and nation-building.

---

8   For instance, Liang Qichao (梁启超) published one long article on two newspaper issues to advocate enlightened thoughts imported from the West: he did not only urge for liberty and equality to replace China's hierarchy and social values, but explicitly expressed that China's revitalization could only be realized via properly educated young people and children. As a result, 1905 saw the Imperial Examination System (*Keju*, 科举) abolished, giving way to universal education along Western lines (see Wu Qinan 114; Wang Lei 41).

9   Traditionally, Chinese literature acknowledged no such thing as "children's literature", and whatever literary education there was for children in imperial China was largely limited to Confucian classics, which paved the way to imperial examinations through which China's bureaucratic administrators were selected and cultural unity and consensus of the country sustained.

Since the mid-19th century, Western notions of children and children's education – such as those advocated by Comenius, Locke, and Rousseau – had been introduced into China. The Romantic period in Europe reshaped the West's conceptualization of the child as endowed with native genius, talent, and imagination, which education must accordingly further nourish. Meanwhile, notions of childhood also arose out of its fascination with democracy, change, and renewal.[10] In discussing the historical and connotative dimensions of the rise of "children's literature", Deborah Cogan Thacker and Jean Webb observe that the construction of childhood in an age of revolution and reform is "neither a politically disinterested nor an ideologically neutral matter" (19); the same can be said of China's re-conceptualization of childhood and the child.

As foreign aggressors and domestic warlords continued to plague the young republican China, enlightened elites campaigned for the New Culture Movement (1915-19), called for democracy and science, challenged Confucian dogmatism, and imported Marxist Socialism. In the arena of culture and amid various agendas, the New Culture Movement urged the replacement of classical Chinese with Plain Words (白话), i.e. common people's language, the vernacular. Hu Shi (胡适), eminent translator, social thinker, educator and writer, published "On the Reform of Literature" (《文学改良刍议》, 1917) in *La Jeunesse* (*New Youth*, 《新青年》), the avant-garde publication and mouthpiece of the New Culture Movement, in which the use of plain words was urged as emancipatory for individual character and freedom of thought. Shi's advocacy soon snowballed into a literary-cultural revolution, supported by pre-eminent intellectuals and co-leaders of this movement, among whom were Zhou Zuoren, Luxun, and Liu Bannong, loyal fans of Andersen. In addition to political and socio-cultural polemics, *La Jeunesse* published Zhou's harsh criticism on the first collection of Andersen's tales in China which, as it was rendered in literary Chinese, "failed to do Andersen justice" in Zhou's view.[11] To drive his point home, in the next issue of *La Jeunesse* (1919, Vol. 6, No. 1) Zhou published his plain-Chinese translation of "The Little Match Girl" (Wang Lei 211).

---

10 For instance, Rousseau's *Emile* (1762) presented a revolutionary, but simple, view that celebrated the natural tendencies of childhood and demanded that they be celebrated and nurtured, rather than directed towards adult values and knowledge.

11 "Random Thoughts", first published in *La Jeunesse*, 1918, Vol. 5, No. 3 (Wang Quangen, *Andersen Research* 8-13; my translation). Adding fuel to Zhou's fire, this first collection of Andersen's tales presented the author of these tales as "The Englishman Andersen".

The May Fourth Movement, the culmination of New Culture Movement, was a patriotic demonstration condemning European Imperialism and China's intransigent conservatism. China's modernization project "rediscovered" the child: Children's nature – thought to be imaginative, innocent, sometimes mischievous, and susceptible to a sense of nonsense – must be recognized in order to bring out the best of their potential – which the May Fourth Movement promptly did.[12] Both Zhou Zuoren and Luxun were instrumental in ushering in the modernized notion of children. Zhou, in particular, developed the theory that books for children must be written in accord with their nature – this view has come to dominate China's world of children's literature under the name of "child-centerism". Zhou marked Andersen's artistic achievement as the accessibility of language and the fantastical sense of nonsense/imagination unhampered by morality (Zhou Zuoren, "Random Thoughts"; Wang Quangen, *Andersen Research* 8-13). Zhou sees children's literature as identical to fairy tales, the kind the Brothers Grimm and Andersen produced. Zhou's theorisation quickly kindled scholarly ardour and creative imitation in young writers, some of whom became important Andersen translators in the ensuing decades.[13] The 1920s in China witnessed the mushrooming of Andersen translations and collections of fairy tales. The influence of Andersen in China had spread so rapidly that in 1925, to commemorate this writer's 120th anniversary and under the editorship of Zheng Zhenduo, *The Short Story Magazine* (《小说月报》) dedicated two monthly issues to Andersen (Vol. XVI, No. 8 and 9), in addition to the discussion and introduction on Andersen's fairy tales in *Literature Weekly* (《文学周报》, No. 186),[14] both periodicals being China's leading trend-setters for high literature.

The New Culture Movement and the May Fourth Movement both saw Andersen primarily as a Romantic, rather than a *romancer* (fabulist/fantasist). Andersen's tales were remarkable in their freshness of

---

12 In exactly the same historical context of crises, the category of "woman" was redefined to be a viable component of society, rather than being merely an unnamed person of subjugation. The enlightened view of a modern woman helped liberate Chinese women from their physical constraints – feet-binding and chest-binding; and schools were set up to formally educate daughters of middle-class gentlemen.

13 For instance, Zheng Zhenduo (郑振铎, 1898-1958) and Ye Junjian (叶君健, 1914-99) were authoritative Andersen translators as well as significant writers of children's stories. They were noteworthy literary scholars and educators.

14 Li Hongye, *Chinese Interpretations* 51-52. For the translation and publication of Andersen's fairy tales in early 20th century China, Wang Lei's book has a useful appendix.

language and their novelty. Young republican China freely embraced such tales that signalled innovation and radical change. After 1919, all translations and responses to Andersen and his works were to be written in plain Chinese to draw this plain-speaking writer closer to an expanding readership. Accordingly, "children's literature" in Chinese language has become synonymous with "fairy tale" (童话) – a lexico-cultural confusion *and* conflation persisting even to this day.[15] The May Fourth Movement consolidated Andersen's status as a romantic writer of fairy tales; this view would always prevail, yet in the face of forthcoming tribulations, China's post-1920s reception of Andersen was to be further entangled with the nation's political imperatives.

III. A Historical Overview of China's Reception of Hans Christian Andersen: How Andersen Studies in China Became Studies of Children's Literature

1920s to early 1930s: Andersen as a Romantic Humanist
The 1920s witnessed China's Andersen-translation boom, which peaked in 1925, yielding more than 90 translated tales and 15 introductory or biographical accounts, many of which appeared in *The Short Story Magazine* and *Literature Weekly*.[16] Andersen translation, in the 1920s, encouraged the rise of many writers of children's literature, many of whom were themselves established translators either of Andersen or of fairy tales.[17] In the 1920s and early 1930s China continued to see Andersen as a Romantic genius. However, as China found itself subject to intensifying foreign aggression and domestic distress, Andersen's

---

15 The original term in Chinese for "literature for children", in Sun's use, was *tonghua* 童话, "children's words / stories for children", which he used to cover both realistic and non-realistic writings suitable for children. In Zhou's theorization of this category, which stemmed from an anthropological perspective, this term was taken to mean non-realistic stories such as folktales and fairy tales. We may take it that Sun used the term in its broadest sense, and Zhao in its narrowest. Chinese scholars of children's literature have pointed out that it was the introduction into China of Western fairy tales since the early 20th century that spurred the rise of China's children's literature *per se*. In this newly-charted realm, Hans Christian Andersen was – and has been – recognized as the most significant influence (Wang Lei 88-92; Wu Qinan 130-134).
16 Observation of Zheng Zhenduo, 1924; Li Hongye *Chinese Interpretations*, 92.
17 Chinese Fairy tale writers who were translators of Andersen's tales or/and influenced by them include Zheng Zhenduo, Mao Dun (茅盾, 1896-1981), Ye Shengtao (叶圣陶, 1894-1988), and Zhao Jingshen (赵景深, 1902-85) (Wu Qi-Nan 152-181).

tales started to take on a humanist/humanitarian overtone. For instance, in Zhao Jingshen's discussion of the thoughts in Andersen's fairy tales, "The Candles", when read metaphorically, made a universalizing statement: "there is no difference between the rich and the poor in nature, no-one is nobler, or baser, than the other. All are equal." Zhao further argued that, in Andersen's fairy tales, more memorable than the childish features are the depictions of human qualities such as patriotism, self-sacrifice, bravery, and perseverance (Li Hongye, *Chinese Interpretations* 72, 78. My translation).

1930s to 1940s: Andersen as a Social Satirist
Children, both collectively and as individuals, are often at the centre of pragmatic debates about education and the inculcation of moral values. The appearance of the leftist literature in the 1930s caused China's children's literature to shift – from its previous Romantic foci of individuality and imagination – to social immediacy and educational usefulness (Li Hongye *Chinese Interpretations*, 105-112). Though still revered as a great children's writer, Andersen (and the kind of fairy tales he and his followers represented) was thought by some Chinese intellectuals of the 1930s to be "far too fantastical to be of any practical good to China's problems." At its most severe, criticism of fantasy and the rhetoric of personification were merciless (Wu Qinan 189. My translation). In 1935, the famous writer Mao Dun (茅盾) openly stated that the most typical feature of Andersen's fairy tales is their escapism – that "they shy away from reality and hide in a paradise of swans and mermaids." (Li Hongye, "Serious Insufficiency". My translation). The harshness of this comment, in my view, directly addressed the imminence and gravity of China's nationhood at peril, particularly against the background of the impending Second Sino-Japanese War (1937-45) which would soon extensively engulf the whole of China for eight long, pain-stricken years.

Opposing views, however, stated that in spite of their highly improbable flights of fancy, Andersen's fairy tales were indeed rooted in the writer's social reality: that they can be read metonymically as social satires. If the 1920s and early 1930s read Andersen's tales as child-centred in their demonstration of nonsensical humour and imagination, the 1940s critics argued that some of these tales – such as "The Little Match Girl" and "The Tinderbox" – offer allegories of social ills. Such a change of interpretation led to a still on-going debate: Should the nature of children's literature be child-centred *only*? Should children read only those fantastic works that are remote from social reality, or be encouraged to get a glimpse of the issues of violence, oppression, and corruption in society? Chinese critics of the 1940s took the latter view.

For instance, Ye Shengtao, as China's first native-born writer of fairy tales, rewrote "The Emperor's New Clothes" and politicized its original concern with universal human nature (the emperor was merely a silly, vain old man) to allude to fascist tyranny and its inevitable downfall in the collective presence of the people. Similarly, "The Little Match Girl" came to represent the oppressed, exploited underclass (Li Hongye, *Chinese Interpretations* 121, 131). Such an interpretive turn signalled the politicization of Andersen within China's specific contexts and the birth of a new genre practised by Chinese writers of children's literature: political fairy tales (Wu Qinan 190-214).

1950s to 1970s: Andersen as a Proletarian Polemist
The first decade after the establishment of the People's Republic of China in 1949 saw another upsurge in Andersen translation. Previous translations of Andersen's tales were largely based on the English, French or Japanese editions of the original; in the 1950s, however, Ye Junjian worked on a new series of Andersen's tales directly from the Danish. Ye's translation is known for its poeticism and thematic faithfulness, though it tends to perceive these tales as reflecting Andersen's own experiences or/and in terms of Marxist political theories. Andersen, as Ye commented on several occasions, "is a great realist of 19th century Denmark" and the two predominant themes of his tales are his assault on the brutal, oppressive ruling class and his sympathy with the proletariat (Li Hongye, *Chinese Interpretations* 139-141). This official view was repeated by multiple print-media: regional newspapers, elementary literacy-promotion publications, and academic publications of teacher training colleges. It became mandatory for children's literature to "reflect political movements and the social construction of socialism; it must advance children's character-forming and moral values." (Wu Qinan 235. My translation). Andersen, in the 1950s, became a proletarian polemist.[18] Class oppression and sympathy for

---

18 For instance, Chen Bochui (陈伯吹), a scholar of Andersen and children's literature, enthusiastically expressed this view in his essays on Andersen's tales accompanied by

the underdog became the keynote of the mid-20th century Chinese interpretation of Andersen's fairy tales. Heavily politicized, even Andersen's life is made to yield a moralizing fable of class-struggle (Qian Zhongli, "Andersen's Fairy Tales" 144-150). In addition, given China's avowed official stance of atheism, Christian meanings that take up a preponderant role in many of Andersen's tales were either ignored, or generalized as humanitarian issues, or simply glossed over in terms of class conflicts. Thus pinned down, Andersen was re-formed and criticized. Ye condescendingly observed that, despite this writer's disclosure of social problems and his hope for future societal amendment, Andersen failed to see the correct direction for social development and wrongly sought solace in Christian determinism (Li Hongye, *Chinese Interpretations* 143). In other words, Andersen is here being consigned to a Marxist limbo because he did not seem to be fully aware of the gospel of the *Communist Manifesto*.

In China, Andersen's tales have been subject to interpretive manipulation which – in Li's concepts as rendered by my literalization – amounts to *childization* ("being made to appear child-like", 儿童化) and *Chinazation* ("being made to fit Chinese standards or appear Chinese", 中国化).[19] This means that Hans Christian Andersen and his fairy tales, though immortalized and highly acclaimed in China, nevertheless suffer from infantilization, as they were interpreted from a perspective designed to exclusively cater for China's socio-political needs. The above historical review of Andersen's reception in China testifies to this phenomenon. Throughout the 1960s and much of the 1970s, virtually all creative and critical energies in China were politically orchestrated. In the late 1970s, as the country slowly picked itself up, Andersen scholars appeared to be a little unsure of how to handle fairy tales and Andersen. In a 1978 essay marking the re-issuing of

---

references to Lenin and other Soviet writers. Two of Chen Bochui's essays on Andersen ("What Do We Learn From Andersen," *People's Daily*, 2 April, 1955; and "Commentary on Andersen's Art: In Commemoration of the 150th Anniversary of Andersen's Birth," *Da Gong Newspaper*, 5 May, 1955) are included in Wang Quangen's book, *Andersen Research* 69-82.

19 Concepts quoted in Li Hongye, *Chinese Interpretations* 175. Assoc. On reading a previous draft of this paper, Kyoo Lee, associate professor of John Jay College, CUNY, NY, USA, suggested a standard and arguably familiar expression for these two concepts: *infantilization* and *sinofication*. However, as we both agreed that *sinofication* comes with a cognitive implication predominantly related to ancient China and its culture, rather than giving a temporal closeness to post-19th century China, I decided to keep to the alliterative, if awkward, literal coinages of *childization* and *Chinazation*. My gratitude to Kyoo Lee.

Andersen's fairy tales, Jin Jin (金近) employed a "merry-go-round" approach that encompasses various critical views of Andersen's fairy tales: Andersen was a fabulist like the Brothers Grimm, a silly old bachelor of remarkable imagination and artistic talent, and a realist for the under-classes. Jin's conclusion clearly indicates China's eclectic interpretative manipulation of Andersen:

> [S]ome of Andersen's later works are less optimistic and positive than his early works; they are disillusioned, passive, even pessimistic, with his characteristic fantasy and humour diminished. This observation is true, and Andersen's change was closely related to the kind of social reality he then witnessed. With his religious pietism, it is impossible for him to arrive at a correct understanding of the world. [...] Therefore, in order to cater for the different reading capacities of children and adults, it is necessary that selective collections and complete collected works of his be separately published.[20]

Jin's remark hints at both a pedagogical function of Andersen's fairy tales and a Political Correctness imperative in the dissemination of his works. Defining Andersen as primarily a children's writer, this commentary discloses an intricate web of signification involving the production of knowledge and the exercise of power.

As China began to open up and reform and its higher education became re-institutionalized, Andersen Studies arose to chart out a territory of its own. Wang Quangen's essay of 1981 discusses the aesthetic features of Andersen's fairy tales, which he summed up as truthfulness to life, innovation of the folktale genre, novelty of thought and language, and beauty of humanity.[21] Both Jin's and Wang's views of Andersen have achieved consensus in China, thus consolidating Andersen's canonical position in the field of modern Chinese literature which includes children's literature/and education, and comparative literature. Thereafter, China's Andersen scholarship largely employs a biographical reading to identify Andersen's tales with his life, a humanist approach to highlight this writer's imaginativeness, the aes-

---

20 Jin Jin, 金近, 1915-89, influential scholar and writer of children's literature. Jin Jin, "The Achievement of Andersen's Fairy tales", Wang Quangen, *Andersen Research* 103-110, 110 (my translation).
21 Wang Quangen, "On the Aestheticism of Andersen's Fairy tales," *Andersen Research*, 127-150.

thetic qualities of his writing, the sublimity/beauty of humanity, and a humanitarian interpretation to explicate the moral stand and sympathy many of Andersen's tales adopt towards the underprivileged, marginalized classes.

IV. "The Little Mermaid" in Contemporary China

Academically speaking, Andersen studies in China bridge the fields of Foreign Literature and Chinese Literature. However, given the long-standing history of Andersen translation and scholarship in China, Andersen Studies in China tend to pivot around *childization* and *Chinazation*: they have become distinctly associated with children's literature in China. Curious about how present-day Chinese scholars read "The Little Mermaid", I attempted a survey of Chinese scholarly commentaries by accessing the Wang-Fan Scholarly Publication Database (万方数据平台学术期刊论文库, http://d.g.wanfangdata.com.cn/Periodical, 2012-08-12), a comprehensive database of Chinese scholarly publications, in which I searched for all literary periodical publications from 1995 to 2012 bearing the Chinese equivalent of "The Little Mermaid" ("海的女儿"). The search yields 196 hits.

A breakdown of this total of 196 gives:

Repeated entry	1
Irrelevant entry[22]	118
Relevant entry	77

Only the 77 relevant entries are of use for my survey and they can further be broken down into essays of a scholarly nature as published in China's higher education academic journals: 33

---

22 As is known, an on-line search engine does not differentiate in terms of the nature of its findings, but simply presents all hits in which the key-words occur. Hence, many irrelevant articles inevitably turn up, such as one account in *Management and Wealth* (2004) introducing a successful woman-entrepreneur who is a "daughter of the sea" (i.e. from a seaside village). Another article, in *Food and Health* (2007), has the wording of "The Little Mermaid" in its elaboration on the Nordic fishing industry. Hits like these are irrelevant to my inquiry and have been dismissed.

| Journal of Teacher Training College/College of Education | 16 |
| Journal of some other types of colleges | 17 |

and essays of a popularizing and/or educational nature: 44

published in literary magazines or quasi-scholarly journals	15
written by school pupils or as school-level literary reference	18
as pre-school pictorial reading	11

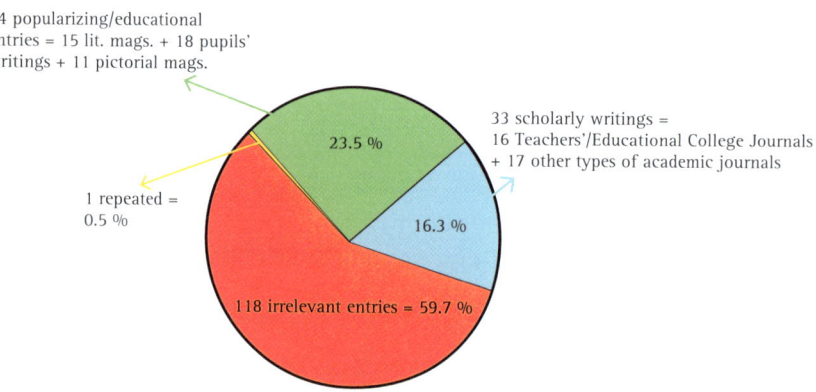

Among findings relevant to "The Little Mermaid", a distinction can be drawn regarding the nature of these publications: Scholarly essays (16.3%) and Educational/Popularizing writings (23.5%).

First, a brief analysis of these relevant entries in terms of the nature of journals that publish them and their intended readership. Nearly half of the 33 scholarly entries which are recognized as academic essays (16) are published in journals of China's various Teacher Training Colleges or Colleges of Education, and the other half (17) in academic journals of either technical institutes or comprehensive higher educational institutions. This indicates a marked receptivity of Normal Universities, Teacher Training Colleges and Colleges of Education *towards* writings on/about "The Little Mermaid".

Among the 44 Educational/Popularizing entries, 15 have been written by scholars and published in literary magazines, 18 are pupils' appreciative comments, and 11 are pictorial renderings for pre-school kids. This shows the popularity of "The Little Mermaid" among common readers as well as school-level readers. From these two observations it is safe to note that "The Little Mermaid" is deemed to be of high educational value and is popular at all pre-college levels.

I then read through the various responses and compositions by school pupils as found in this search: largely written by girls, they uniformly point out the virtues the little mermaid exhibits – her compassion for and loyalty to the prince, her endurance of physical pain and perseverance in pursuing happiness, in particular, her self-sacrifice and all-embracing love. For these young readers, this is a moral(ising) story: you must strive for happiness and cultivate a noble ideal of life; when in love you must be considerate towards the well-being of the beloved and if necessary set aside your own interests. Self-abnegation is the highest manifestation of love, obviously and especially for girls, which is the unspoken and un-reflected-on subtext many young readers of this tale subscribe to.[23] Such correspondence uncannily echoes the view of Marcia Lieberman that fairy tales are a source of female acculturation, that they give us "an insight into some of the origins of [women's] psycho-sexual identity" (384).

Next I delved into essays penned by adults, including all 33 academic essays and those 15 pieces in literary magazines. These essays about "The Little Mermaid", 48 in total, embody China's literary interest and endeavour, inside and outside the higher education compass. From 1995 to 2012, China's prestigious journals (CSSCI-indexed) published 4 critical essays on/about "The Little Mermaid",[24] so it is clear that this story has been studied critically. The remaining, however, fluctuate discernibly in quality as well as focus.

---

23 I relied on my common sense to determine the sex of these juvenile writers from the hints embedded in their names. Yet, for their privacy, I choose here not to disclose these names and specific personal information. However, for the overall gist, we may refer to some titles of these appreciative writings: "Persevering for an Immortal Soul: Reading 'The Little Mermaid'" ("坚持，为了一个不灭的灵魂——读《海的女儿》有感"), or "Bravely Go After Happiness: After Reading 'The Little Mermaid'" ("要勇敢追求幸福——读《海的女儿》有感"), or "A Myth: On Reading 'The Little Mermaid'" ("神话——读《海的女儿》有感"). These titular translations are mine.

24 Please find in the list provided below these four CSSCI indexed essays as sequenced 3 ("Subtraction Principle of Andersen's Fairy Tales"), 76 ("The mermaid's love: On similar love motive in stories by Andersen, Zweig, and Bunin", Translation mine.), 80 ("On the Tragic Psychology of Anders[e]n in Writing His Fairy Tales"), and 85 ("Western Archetypal Criticism and the Biblical Archetypes in Andersen's Fairy Tales").

Sequence No. in Database, (*General Lit. Mag.)	Chinese Title	English Title (as given in original, unless * to mark my translation)	Key Points	Author Type
Individual Entries					
1	《海的女儿》的多种解读可能，韦苇，《昆明师范高等专科学校学报》，2005, 27 (3), 1-12	"Multiple Interpretations of 'The Little Sea Maid'", Wei Wei, *Journal of Kunming Teachers College*, 2005, 27 (3), 1-12	Humanist and biographical approaches	Children's lit. scholar
2	《海的女儿》的酷儿解读，付飞亮，《湖南科技学院学报》，2008 29 (9), 15-17	"A Queer Reading of 'The Little Mermaid'", Fu Feiliang, *Journal of Hunan University of Science and Engineering*, 2008 29 (9), 15-17	Gaze theory, androgyny	Chinese/ Comparative lit. scholar
13 *	论《海的女儿》中关于红色的隐喻，彭应翃，《理论界》，2008, 7, 126-127	(*) "On the Metaphor of the Color Red in 'The Little Mermaid'", Peng Yinghong, *Theory Horizon*, 2008, 7, 126-127	Red as symbol of passion, self-sacrifice, and spiritual devotion	Chinese/ Comparative lit. scholar
16	《海的女儿》的三重世界及其"生命之痛"的启蒙意蕴，陈刚，《海南广播电视大学学报》，2004, No.4, 11-13	(*) "The Triplex World of 'The Little Mermaid' and its Enlightened Meaning", Chen Gang, *Journal of Hainan Radio and TV University*, 2004, No. 4, 11-13	Ascension, enlightenment	Chinese lit. scholar
38	无法通过的"通过仪式"——《海的女儿》的文化人类学解读，刘彩珍，《通化师范学院学报》，2005, 26 (3), 101-104	"A Failure of Rites of Passage: The anthropology interpretation of 'The Little Mermaid'", Liu Caizhen, *Journal of Tonghua Teachers' College*, 2005, 26 (3), 101-104	Anthropology, rites of passage	Chinese lit. MA scholar
86*	童话背后，是怎样的安徒生？，翟维纳，《出版广角》，2011 (4), 64	(*) "What is Andersen Like Behind his Fairy Tales?", Zhai Weina, *View of Publishing*, 2011 (4), 64	Briefing of the re-translated issue (2011) of Andersen's *My Life as a Fairy tale*	?

45	谈文学作品中的异类变身形象，曹迁平，陈宇，《九江学院学报》，2004, 4, 54-57	(*) "Metamorphosis in Literature", Cao Qianping, Chen Yu, *Journal of Jiujiang University*, 2004, 4, 54-57	Comparison with Chinese folktale, *Lei-Feng Tower*	Foreign lit. scholar
48	安徒生童话人物结构分类模式解析，时翠萍，《淮海工学院学报（人文社科版）》，2003, 1 (4), 19-20	"The Character-classifying Modes in H. C. Andersen's Fairy Tales", Shi Cuiping, *Journal of Huaihai Institute of Technology (Humanities & Social Sciences Edition)*, 2003, 1 (4), 19-20	Introduction via basic structuralistic narratology	Elementary education scholar
85	西方传统中的原型批评与安徒生童话的圣经批评，顾悦，《江苏社会科学》，2011 (3), 182-186	(*) "Western Archetypal Criticism and Biblical Archetypes in Andersen's Fairy Tales", Gu Yue, *Jiangsu Social Science*, 2011 (3), 182-186	With 4 English references; thematic interpretation of redemption	CSSCI; Foreign lit. PhD scholar
11	从《龙王公主》和《海的女儿》看中西文化的不同表现，陈元元，《安徽科学院学报》，2008, 22 (1), 87-90	"The Difference between Chinese Culture and Western Culture in *The Dragon King's Daughter* and *The Little Mermaid*", Chen Yuanyuan, *Journal of Anhui Science and Technology University*, 2008, 22 (1), 87-90	Senior-junior ethical relation, attitudes of love and marriage, educational difference	Foreign lit. MA scholar
120*	诗意世界中的童话——安徒生和王尔德童话诗意美之比较，黄俏，《陕西教育》，2008 (5), 64	(*) "A Comparative Study of Andersen's and Wilde's Fairytale Aesthetics", Huang Qiao, *Shanxi Education*, 2008 (5), 64	Introduction to the art of Andersen's and Wilde's fairy tales	Chinese/Comparative lit. scholar
	Grouped Entries of Similar Foci (in chronological sequence)			
4	人类中心意识下的异类悲剧——《海的女儿》寓言解析，胡红，《昭通师范高等专科学校学报》，2004, 26 (4), 16-20	"A Tragedy of the Alien Class from the Human Center of Consciousness – An Allegorical Analysis of 'The Little Mermaid' by H. C. Andersen", Hu Hong, *Journal of Zhaotong Teacher's College*, 2004, Vol. 26, No.4, 16-20	Plot-based retelling, alienation and human-centrism	Chinese/Comparative lit. scholar

15	《海的女儿》中小人鱼形象的人类中心意识解读，吴东，《湖南人文科技学院学报》，2007 (5), 23-26	"Explanation on the Mankind Center of Consciousness of The Little Mermaid in Sea's Daughter", Wu Dong, *Journal of Hunan Institute of Humanities, Science and Technology*, 2007 (5), 23-26	Same as (or appearing unaware of) the above/4	Chinese/Comparative lit. scholar
14*	不可逾越的鸿沟——《海的女儿》的生态批评解读，吴东，《天中学刊》，2008, 23 (1), 64-67	"An Impassable Gulf – the Eco-critic Reading of *The Little Mermaid*", Wu Dong, *Journal of Tianzhong*, 2008, 23 (1), 64-67	Essay identical with the above/15. Virtually the same essay published twice with different titles	Chinese/Comparative lit. scholar
55	试论《海的女儿》中的自我象征性，李树为，《牡丹江师范学院学报（哲社版）》，2002 (4), 35-36	(*) "Symbolism of Self in 'The Little Mermaid'", Li Shuwei, *Journal of Mudanjiang Teachers College (Social Sicences)*, 2002 (4), 35-36	Plot-based retelling	?
44	爱在人间——读安徒生童话《海的女儿》，卢坤甫，《乌鲁木齐成人教育学院学报》，2004, 12(4)	"Love in the Human World – From Antusheng's Tale 'The Sea Daughter'", *Journal of Urumqi Adult Education Institute*, 2004, 12(4)	Plot-based retelling	Foreign lit. scholar
21	潜藏的激流——论《海的女儿》及安徒生的生命意识，周笑海，《浙江师范大学学报（社科版）》，2004, 29 (6), 11-15	"A Torrent beneath: On 'The Little Sea Maid' and Andersen's Life Consciousness", Zhou Xiaohai, *Journal of Zhejiang Normal University (Social Sciences)*, 2004, 29 (6), 11-15	Humanist discussion of TLM in relation to the Bildungsroman, Kierkegaard	Chinese/Comparative lit. MA scholar
10*	诗意的生命存在——《海的女儿》中女主人公形象探析，张微，王东星，《语文学刊》，2009, No.12, 122-123	(*) "Poetic Existence: On the Characterization of 'The Little Mermaid'", Zhang Wei, Wang Dongxing, *Journal of Language and Literature Studies*, 2009, Nos. 12, 122-123	General humanistic appraisal	Chinese/Comparative lit. MA scholar

31	安徒生作品之《海的女儿》解析，程林超，《南昌教育学院学报》，2010, 25 (5), 21	"Analysis of the Andersen work 'The Daughter of the Sea'", Cheng Linchao, *Journal of Nanchang College of Education*, 2010, 25 (5), 21	Plot-based retelling, humanistic appraisal	Elementary Education scholar
18	不灭的赞歌——从《海的女儿》分析安徒生爱的意识，唐娟，《湖南科技学院学报》，2012, 33(1), 28-30	(*) "Analysis of Love in 'The Little Mermaid'", Tang Juan, *Journal of Hunan University of Science and Engineering*, 2012, 33(1), 28-30	Plot-based retelling, humanistic appraisal	Officer of local cultural dept.
25*	浅谈《海的女儿》中小人鱼的形象，谢全霞，《文艺生活.文海艺苑》，2012 九月, 12, 14	"On Characterization of 'The Little Mermaid'", Xie Qianxia, *Literary Gallery*, 2012 Sept., 12, 14	Plot-based retelling, humanistic appraisal	Pre-school Education scholar
30	安徒生"海的女儿"文学形象原型考析，唐均，杨天舒，《湘潭师范学院学报《社科版》》，2001, Vol. 23, No. 6, 86-90	"An Analysis on Mythic Prototype and Literary Conception of the Heroine in H. C. Andersen's The Little Mermaid", Tang Jun, Yang Tianshu, *Journal of Xiangtan Normal University (Social Science Edition)*, 2001, Vol. 23, No. 6, 86-90	Folkloric origin of the mermaid, Undine	Chinese/Comparative lit. scholars
3	重新寻找安徒生童话的源头——《海的女儿》来自对《温婷娜》的传承和创新，唐池子，《上海师范大学学报（社科版）》, 2005, 34 (5), 100-106	"The Subtraction Principle of Andersen's Fairy Tales", Tang Chizi, *Journal of Shanghai Normal University (Philosophy & Social Science Edition)*, 2005, 34 (5), 100-106	Intertextual influence between Undine and The Little Mermaid; unaware of the above/30	CSSCI; Children's lit. scholar

22	爱，是使灵魂飞往天国的翅膀——《海的女儿》与《打渔人和他的灵魂》之比较，孔凡飞，《昆明师范高等专科学校学报》, 2004, 26 (3), 27-30	"Love Enables Your Spirit to Take Wing to Paradise – The Comparison between *The Daughter of the Sea* and *The Fisherman and His Soul*", Kong Fanfei, *Journal of Kunming Teachers College*, 2004, 26 (3), 27-30	Comparison with Wilde	Foreign lit. scholar
8	爱与美的哀歌——《海的女儿》与《打渔人和他的灵魂》之比较，彭应翊，《文教资料》, 2010 (1), 24-26	(*) "Elegy of Love and Beauty: A Comparison between *The Daughter of the Sea* and *The Fisherman and His Soul*", Peng Yinghong, *Data of Culture and Education*, 2010 (1), 24-26	Critical concern same as – yet unaware of – the above/22	Chinese/Comparative lit. scholar
7	点点滴滴皆童趣——论迪斯尼动画片《小美人鱼》对《海的女儿》的改编，王会敏，《兰州教育学院学报》, 2010, Vol. 26, NO. 3, 16-18	(*) "On How Disney's *The Little Mermaid* Changes Andersen's *The Little Mermaid*", Wang Huiming, *Journal of Lanzhou Education College*, 2010, Vol. 26, NO. 3, 16-18	Differences in medium, themes, conflicts, characterization, endings, etc.	Liberal Arts scholar
17*	经典文本《海的女儿》的拼贴与重组，程瑜瑜，《电影文学》, 2010 (13), 31-34	(*) "Pastiche and Re-assemblage: on Disney's 'The Little Mermaid'", Cheng Yuyu, *Movie Literature*, 2010 (13), 31-34	Unaware of 7. Uses foreign language resources	Foreign lit. scholar
121*	成人动画与儿童动画：《小美人鱼》与《悬崖上的金鱼公主》比较研究，冯晓雯，《电影评介》, 2012 (1), 76-77	(*) "A Comparison of 'Ponyo on the Cliff and 'The Little Mermaid': on animation films for grownups and those for children", Feng Xiaowen, *Movie Review*, 2012 (1), 76-77	Partly the same as 7?	?

51	自卑与超越——再读《丑小鸭》和《海的女儿》，韦晓瑛，《南京晓庄学院学报》, 2003, 19(3), 54-57	"Inferiority Complex and surmounting: Re-reading 'Ugly Duckling' and 'Daughter of the Sea'", Wei Xiaoying, *Journal of Nanjing Xiaozhuang College*, 2003, 19(3), 54-57	Alienation, assimilation, passion of life/love, humanist reading	Chinese/Comparative lit. scholar
53	跨越时空的吟唱——从《丑小鸭》和《海的女儿》看安徒生童话的现代意识，杨宁，《赣南师范学院学报》, 2004, 5, 65-67	"Songs Across the Times: Modern Consciousness in 'The Ugly Duckling' and 'The Little Mermaid'", Yangning, *Journal of Gannan Teachers College*, 2004, 5, 65-67	Character types in folklore, love and fate, humanistic reading	Children's lit. scholar
77*	论童话中的"残酷"叙事与幼儿阅读，金莉莉，《学前教育研究》, 2003, 10, 12-14	(*) "On Violent Narrative in Fairy tale and Children's Reading", Jin Lili, *Studies in Pre-School Education*, 2003, 10, 12-14	Violence, children's education, child psychology	Chinese/Comparative lit. PhD scholar
92*	用安徒生的作品培养儿童的道德情感，李英，《青海教育》, 2005 (7), 47	(*) "Use Andersen's works to cultivate children's moral feelings", Li Ying, *Qinghai Education*, 2005 (7), 47	Acculturation, compassion, selflessness	?
19	美丽的想象，深邃的内涵——从《海的女儿》和《卖火柴的小女孩》看图像时代的儿童阅读，邹敏，《中华女子学院学报》, 2006, 18(6), 68-70	"Colorful Fantasy and Deep Implication: Comprehend Children's Literature in the Visual Era from 'The Little Mermaid' and 'The Little Match Girl'", Zou Min, *Journal of China Women's University*, 2006, 18(6), 68-70	Aesthetic imagination, visual culture, humanistic concerns	Pre school Education scholar
56*	从《海的女儿》看安徒生童话的教化功能，藏凌瑞，《教育时空》, 2012, 9, 219-220	(*) "On the Educational Function of Andersen's Fairy tales: the Case of 'The Little Mermaid'", Zang Lingrui, *China Science and Technology Review*, 2012, 9, 219-220	Fairy tale as educational tool: emotion, aesthetics, humanity, imagination	?

132 *	从两则童话看女性失语，李珊珊，《现代语文》，2007 (4), 79-80	(*) "Speechless Women: 'The Little Mermaid' and 'Wild Swans'", Li Shanshan, *Modern Chinese*, 2007 (4), 79-80	Undine, silencing of women	?
26	女儿只应天上有——以性别史学观品读《海的女儿》，周萍，《辽宁教育行政学院学报》，2008 (1), 153-154	(*) "Gender Poetics and 'The Little Mermaid'", Zhou Ping, *Liaoning College of Education Journal*, 2008 (1), 153-154	Feminism, gender perspective	?
12 *	在沉默与言说之间——《海的女儿》女性主义解读，彭应翃，《现代语文》，2008 (6), 113-114	(*) "Between Silence and Speech: A Feminist Reading of 'The Little Mermaid'", Peng Yinghong, *Modern Chinese*, 2008 (6), 113-114	Power of speech, feminism, oppression	Chinese/Comparative lit. scholar
5	《海的女儿》的女性主义批评，陈丹，《内江师范学院学报》，2010, 9 (25), 59-62	"The Feminist Criticism of The Little Mermaid", Chen Dan, *Journal of Neijiang Normal University*, 2010, 9 (25), 59-60	Simone de Beauvoir, Helen Cixous	Journalism scholar
9	自由浪花——论安徒生《海的女儿》的女性主义诗学观，崔丹，张颖，《重庆交通大学学报（社科版）》，2012, 12 (1), 71-74	"Liberated Seaspray: Study of Andersen's The Little Mermaid from Feminist Perspective", Cui Dan, Zhang Ying, *Journal of Chongqing Jiaotong University (social science edition)*, 2012, 12 (1), 71-74	Simone de Beauvoir, Helen Cixous, Juliet Mitchell. Critical concerns the same as – but unaware of – the above/5; English references (4/15)	Foreign lit. scholar
76	论爱情故事中的"小人鱼"模式——安徒生，茨威格，浦宁三个相似故事及含意，陆黎雅，《外国文学研究》，2003 (2), 114-119	(*) "The mermaid's love: on similar love motif in stories by Andersen, Zweig, and Bunin", Lu Liya, *Foreign Literature Studies*, 2003 (2), 114-119	Unrequited love, TLM, Zweig's *Letters from an Unknown Woman*; English references	CSSCI Full-length words (7000); Liberal Arts MA scholar

137	"小人鱼"爱情模式浅析，时翠萍，《淮海工学院学报（人文社会科学版）》，2005, 3 (4), 19-21	"Loving Pattern of a 'Little Mermaid'", Shi Cuiping, *Journal of Huaihai Institute of Technology (Humanities and Social Sciences Edition)*, 2005, 3 (4), 19-21	Unrequited love, *TLM*, Zweig. Influenced by 76, identical with 4/7 references	Children's lit. scholar
6*	"海的女儿"化身陌生女人"——两个单恋文本的文化解读，王妮，《青年作家》，2010 (8), 20-21	(*) "Transforming 'The Little Mermaid' to an Unknown Woman", Wangni, *Young Writers*, 2010 (8), 20-21	Unrequited love, TLM, Zweig. Originality dubious	?
83	爱是死亡的超越——析安徒生童话里的死亡意识，程开成，应朝华，《黔东南民族师范高等专科学校学报》，2002, 20 (5), 69-70	(*) "Love Transcends Death: On Death in Andersen's Fairy Tales", Cheng Kaicheng, Ying Chaohua, *Journal of Southeast Guizhou National Teacher's College*, 2002, 20 (5), 69-70	Biographical approach to death in TLM and Andersen's tales	Chinese/ Comparative lit. MA scholar
80	论安徒生童话创作的悲剧心理，王宁，《河北大学学报（哲社版）》，2003, 4(28), 142-144	"On the Tragic Psychology of Andersen in Writing His Fairy Tales", Wang Ning, *Journal of Heibei University (Philosophy and Social Science)*, 2003, 4(28), 142-144.	Biographical approach to the tragic elements in Andersen's tales	CSSCI; Chinese/ Comparative lit. scholar
78	浅析安徒生童话中的悲剧情节，胡璐，梅媛，《四川教育学院学报》，2006, 22(1), 84-86	"An Analysis on Tragic Complex in Andersen's Fairy Tales", Hu Lu, Mei Yuan, *Journal of Sichuan College of Education*, 2006, 22 (1), 84-86	Tragedy and violence, TLM, "The Red Shoes", "The Ugly Duckling"	Translation Studies scholars
87*	论安徒生童话的悲剧意识，兰守亭，陈英，《黑河学刊》，2007, 129(3), 40-42	(*) "On Tragedy in Andersen's Fairy Tales", Lan Shouting, Chen Ying, *Heihe Journal*, 2007, 129(3), 40-42	Biographical approach to the tragic elements in Andersen's tales. Erroneous info. of Andersen's life	Foreign lit. scholar

127	安徒生悲剧童话的审美观照，兰守亭，《西昌学院学报（社科版）》, 2007, 19(3), 36-39	"On The Aesthetic Reviewing of Andersen's Tragic Fairy Tales", Lan Shouting, Journal of Xichang College (Social Science Edition), 2007, 19(3), 36-39	Largely identical with the above/87 by the same author.	Foreign lit. scholar
28	从《海的女儿》探究安徒生悲剧童话的价值，李珂，《琼州学院学报》, 2012, 19(1), 55-56	"Analysis of the Tragedy Value of Andersen's Fairy Tales from 'The Little Mermaid'", Li Ke, *Journal of Qiongzhou University*, 2012, 19(1), 55-56	Biographical approach to identify the little mermaid with Andersen	Foreign lit. scholar

Authorship Composition

10/48 Foreign literature scholars → *Field of Foreign Literary Studies: 21%*

18/48 Chinese/Comparative literature scholars} *Field of Chinese Literary Studies: 52%*

7/48 Children's literature/Education scholars} –

5/48 Others (Translation Studies, Journalism, Liberal Arts, etc.)} *Others: 27%*

8/48 Unknown / Common Readers} –

Analysis of the 48 scholarly essays

- Authorship: A little more than half of the authors (52%) come from the field of Chinese literary studies, which incorporates both Comparative Literature and Children's Literature within its scope. Scholars of Foreign Literary Studies account for only about 21%, leaving 27% to be represented by authors from other fields and/or of an unspecified status. This authorship analysis suggests that "The Little Mermaid" is most often discussed and written about by scholars/students of Chinese Literature, and least so by Foreign Literature scholars.
- Length of essay: Apart from the 4 full-length CSSCI-indexed essays, most papers are only 2-4 pages long, with a word-count (Chinese) of no more than 3000. Such slimness does not accommodate in-depth critical treatment of the tale and inevitably lends an impression of insignificance and superficiality to the tale.

- Critical perspective: Most essays conduct plot-based or theme-based discussion; only a few touch on critical perspectives in their discussion. Those that do, however, feature only a rudimentary level of criticism.
- Research homogeneity: Scholarly and thematic repetition is apparent in these essays; it suggests, on the part of the writer, little awareness of existing scholarship in China, let alone that of the international Andersen Studies community. For instance: numbers 55/44/21/10/31/18/25 all deal with a humanist discussion of selfhood, passion of life, love, and characterization of "The Little Mermaid". Yet curiously, none of the latter shows awareness/acknowledgement of existing scholarship. Also, Nos. 76/137/6 all deal comparatively with "The Little Mermaid" and *Letters from an Unknown Woman*, with 137 using some bibliographical references found in 76; and 6 registers no awareness whatsoever of the other two essays.
- Scope of Resources: The majority of these 48 essays rely on either translated or/and exclusively Chinese scholarship; only 2 essays refer to sources in English. This may suggest a restricted research scope, a disconnectedness between Andersen Studies in China and the international scholarly community.
- Nature of Andersen Studies: The majority of the essays find favour with various journals of normal universities or teachers' colleges; this seems to suggest that, in China, Andersen Studies and Andersen's tales are identified as "children's stuff" – perhaps thereby not serious enough to attract the attention of prestigious literary/academic journals? What is certain is that Andersen's fairy tales elicit more academic interest from the Chinese literature sphere (including Comparative Literature and Children's Literature) than from that of foreign literature. This implies constriction in the nature of China's Andersen Studies.

Updating "The Little Mermaid" Criticism

My research into contemporary scholarly efforts on "The Little Mermaid" in China is a curious and somewhat sour-tasting journey. By no means is it an exhaustive excavation of *all* scholarly and academic endeavours in this regard. My motivation is to gain insight into the ways "The Little Mermaid" is read today. As shown, the predominant scholarly view of "The Little Mermaid" shows a combination of biographical, humanist (Romantic) and humanitarian (socio-realist) approaches, with some exceptions attempting critical approaches such as archetypal, psychoanalytical, feminist, and gender. I applaud this critical turn, because it rescues Andersen's tales from the monolithically moralistic vein that is characteristic of China's children's literature. Yet such critical readings are dated and somewhat redundant because of insufficient scholarly communication and nourishment, if not because of academic and disciplinary close-mindedness.

"The Little Mermaid" is a tale of Christian humility and redemption clothed in a confusing quest narrative. Walt Disney's 1989 release of the animation film of the same name provoked a wave of critical interest. In concluding her 1992 review on this tale, Gwyneth Cravens briefly commented on Disney's film, noting the change of ending and characterization and lamenting the alteration of tone (from sadness to blissfulness) and the thinning of thematic profundity (638-640). Cravens' observations are re-echoed in Finn Hauberg Mortensen's discussion of the iconic aspect of this tale: the mermaid resonates abundantly as a folkloric icon, a bourgeois-Christian icon, and a commercial/*Disneyfied* icon. Informative and cogent, Mortensen's essay gives a rounded analysis of the semiotics of the little mermaid as a symbol and is a valuable reference to readers interested in the cross-medium intertextuality between this tale and its Disney version. Deborah Ross, in her 2004 essay, tackles the fairy tale in relation to gendered imagination, thus adding a feminist/gender perspective to the reading/viewing of "The Little Mermaid" (53-66).

In addition, Pil Dahlerup's 1990 essay deals with various points of confusion and complexity in the tale. What, for example, is the theme of this tale? (420). In the story *per se*, what the little mermaid really wants is to have a soul – which can only be obtainable if she is loved by a human. This mortal *happens* to be the prince, who resembles the boy-statue the little mermaid salvages from a previous shipwreck. Rather than saying that the little mermaid dearly loves the prince, perhaps it makes more sense to say that the prince's love is the means by which the little mermaid can hope to secure immortality. Under the guise of a love narrative, this tale in fact deviates into a quest for redemption, confusing human love with spiritual piety. The ending inserts a bit of evangelical preaching: only when a child fulfils his/her Christian/filial duty will the floating period of the daughters of the air be shortened. Doesn't that – holding children responsible for the moral well-being of the world – amount to emotional/moral blackmail?

In her 1991 essay, Dahlerup enlarged on her deconstructive reading with an examination of other perspectives – the structuralist approach, the psychoanalytic approach, the folktale/Disney approach, the synopsis/humanist reading, and the rhetoric approach. Though Chinese critics of "The Little Mermaid" have attempted all these approaches, none if any has been aware of and benefited from it, let alone able to surpass the penetration of this essay (141-162). In addition, Nancy Easterlin delves into the genealogical history of the mermaid as a symbol, tracing its psycho-cultural extensiveness (251-277). Vivian Yenika-Agbaw, on the other hand, focuses on the issue of disability in relation to Andersen's tales, which is an innovative take to regenerate our appreciation of "The Little Mermaid" (91-97).

Even an unsophisticated feminist reading will note how the mermaid, voiceless and tormented, serves a prince who takes her as a mere play-mate, a pet; this prince is one who never fully appreciates her worth. In my view, a conventional humanist reading – which praises either the little mermaid's consideration and sacrifice for the prince, or her perseverance and devotion in her lofty pursuit (which, I repeat, is immortality, not romantic love *per se*) – is guilty of projecting male-chauvinist wishful thinking. It can be argued that the self-sacrifice of the mermaid and her ultimate suicide are completely out of line with the standards of fairy tales, of children's literature, and (perhaps) of enlightened and emancipated 21st century reality as well. None of the Chinese commentaries from my survey appears to be aware of any of the recent international Andersen critiques I have mentioned – why is that?

V. Dilemmas of Chinese Andersen Studies and Future Prospects

I am fully aware of the limitation in range of this critical attempt. I am aware that it cannot, and does not, fully represent all the scholarly and cultural engagement of Chinese readers/critics of Andersen's works. The main intention of my critique is to warn about current trends, conditions, and methodologies in Andersen studies. Judging from the above study of on-line "Little Mermaid" critiques and commentaries, Andersen Studies in China face the following three dilemmas:

An Incomplete Understanding of Hans Christian Andersen
Though initially Andersen was introduced to China as a poet and a wonder-tale writer, after the 1920s he was soon stuck with the reputation as (only) a fairy tale author for children. This view persists even today. Though updated complete collections of his tales have been published, under the authoritative workmanship of Ye Jun-Jian (from 1950s to 1980s, 叶君健) and Lin Hua (early 1990s, 林桦), general as well as academic understanding of Andersen is still pretty much limited to his few representative tales, leaving much of his other/later tales, such as "Dryad" and "The Shadow", un-heard-of and un-discussed.

Andersen's poems, novels, plays, and poetic travel books are virtually unknown to Chinese readers. Granted that these "serious works" are perhaps only second-rate in the eye of native readers, and that Andersen committed the fault of emotive and expressive excessiveness in his writings for adults,[25] isn't it still profitable for scholars in China to study these in addition to the genre of fairy tale in order to arrive at a fuller cultural understanding of the German-Danish – or the European in general – Romantic movement? Rather than hijacking Andersen exclusively for fairy tales and children, why not expand Andersen studies in China to exploring his *O.T.* and *The Improvisatore* and the early 19th century Romantic Friendship, for instance? How about his dramatic poem, *Agnete and the Merman*, and the semiotic history of European merfolks? To what extent does the Romantic poetics impact on Andersen's own poetry? Of course, to help the world become re-acquainted with Andersen as a versatile writer, and indeed a versatile artist, cultural projects are required to help bring to light more Danish-English translations and discussions of Andersen's lesser-known works in different literary genres and artistic media.

Narrowness of Research Focus and Academic Categorization
The way China's higher education classifies academic disciplines has, in my view, a constraining effect on its Andersen studies. Scholars and

---

25 Commenting on the blatant commercialisation in 2005 that marks Andersen's bicentenary both in Denmark and globally, Stephen Pettitt touches upon an allegedly shared ambivalence of Danish readers and writers towards Hans Christian Andersen. The world's attention to Andersen and his fairy tales has eclipsed his other works, though "[most] Danes who've read them think that they're second-rate, or worse [...]" (56). Similarly, Jackie Wullschlager also mentions that contemporaneous critics of Andersen's early novels and plays commonly thought that Andersen ought to "discipline the fantastical" (102).

students of Chinese literature are completely free to study and write critiques of Andersen's works, even to publish essays on/about him, because Andersen has been integrated into both Comparative Literature and Children's Literature. This is not the case for scholars and students of foreign languages and literatures. At best, Andersen is part of the Nordic literature category, one that is often ruled to be *outside* the nation-based foreign languages and literatures curricula for college majors in foreign languages and literature as devised by the State Education Ministry.[26] An imminent problem resulting from such rigidity of academic demarcation is that Andersen studies in China have little exchange with their international counterpart, whereas scholars of foreign languages and literature are straitjacketed institutionally. Often, scholars of Children's Literature and/or Comparative Literature rely heavily on translation or existing Chinese resources, rather than on materials in foreign languages. Wang Quangen, a leading authority in China's Andersen studies and children's literature, already expresses my misgivings in a preface to a recent monograph on China's Children's Literature: "Due to various reasons – the most noticeable being that this field is in need of scholars who are as proficient in foreign languages as they are knowledgeable in children's literature – China's children's literary studies have had very little exchange with their counterparts abroad." ("Break-through" 1. My translation). Where Wang sighs for Chinese literature for children, I bemoan the dwarfing impact on Andersen and his works if such an arbitrary appropriation continues to dominate Andersen studies in China.

As mentioned, although Ye Junjian and Lin Hua have produced the most reliable translations of Andersen's fairy tales, in the market Andersen's fairy tales have still proliferated in various – and sometimes dubious – translations, rewritings, and excerpted versions; they have snow-balled into assorted picture-books and selected collections,

---

26 My institution is fortunate to house a Center of Nordic Studies, supported under the joint auspices of China and the Nordic countries, to offer courses and promote cultural exchange. In addition, Fudan's College of Foreign Languages and Literature has set up a Research Institute of Nordic Literature which largely relies on its English faculties. According to regulations set forth in "The Syllabus of English Courses for College English Majors", by the National Education Committee, students of English – the majority of foreign languages and literature learners – must write their graduation theses only on Anglo-/American/native English-speaking authors; and English faculties that study Andersen only "do" him on the side. Broadly speaking, although Andersen studies definitely fall into the slot of Foreign Literatures, they are in need of further material, institutional, as well as pedagogical support.

have spawned a progeny of retelling and rewriting. Andersen's representative tales, very much like Shakespeare's *Hamlet*, have become composite tales and the issue of questionable and even unattainable authenticity.

Synoptic Scholarship and Academic Inbreeding

If "monopoly" is too strong a word to apply to Andersen studies in China as Children's Literature Studies, the latter is nevertheless vulnerable to "academic inbreeding", yielding a scholarship that is largely synoptic and mono-focal.[27] Much of China's current Andersen studies relies preponderantly on the works of Wang Quangen and Li Hongye, scholars of modern Chinese literature and children's literature, just as the latter two had depended on Zhou Zuoren, Zheng Zhenduo, Ye Junjian, etc. Recent international Andersen research (works by Maria Tatar, Jack Zipes, and Harold Bloom, to name but a few) and new biographies of Andersen (by Jackie Wullschlager and Jens Andersen, for instance) are relatively unknown in China. Though Jens Andersen's work, known for offering a re-reading of Andersen that is controversially contrary to the self-image Andersen prescribes in his autobiographies, was translated into Chinese in 2005 as a celebratory gesture to mark Hans Christian Andersen's bicentenary, all recent Andersen commentaries I encountered in this research appear oblivious of its existence.[28] Fang Weiping's *Theory of Chinese Children's Literature: A History* (2007), said to be expanded from his 1992 work, does not incorporate any new academic insights other than those already seen in the books by Wang, Li, and Shu. Shu Wei's *In the Wonderland of Fairy Tale* (2011) is enriched by Western critical perspectives on children's literature, such as the inclusion of psychoanalytical paradigms, and discussions of *Lord of the Rings* and *Harry Potter*. Yet, where it deals with Andersen, there is no in-depth discussion of recent, international critical studies and scholarship on Andersen.

---

27 Since the 1980s, Beijing Normal University has become one of China's powerhouses of children's literature and Wang Quangen has played an important role in the recent institutionalization and popularization of this discipline. Li Hongye, Shu Wei, and Wang Lei received their doctorates from this university, possibly under the tutorage of Wang Quangen. In addition, Wang Lei worked as editor for both Wang's and Li's 2005 monographs on Andersen from which hers draws heavily.

28 An exception is met outside this limited survey. Qian Zhongli discusses the Christian imports in Andersen's popular fairy tales and includes in his references the Chinese edition of Jens Andersen's biography of Hans Christian Andersen, without discussing it at all.

This overlooking of recent international Andersen scholarship means that Andersen's autobiographies and earlier biographies are still repeatedly being translated, published, and studied with biblical authority in China. Such an unquestioning, un-critical embrace slants and misguides future scholarly inquiries.[29]

Perspective: the Future for China's Andersen Studies
Freeing this tall lanky writer from his cooped-up nursery status, Andersen Studies have already evolved into an international/ised field of scholarship. In addition to recent biographies, newly disclosed materials and personal papers have also been informing current Andersen commentaries and critiques, many of which are thought-provoking in the Foucauldian dimension – in inviting a self-examination of how one acquires "knowledge" about Hans Christian Andersen.[30]

In China, the public image of Andersen is largely fed by the talespinner's own accounts, on the basis of which a hagiological reading is often applied to Andersen and his works. In stark contrast, recent international studies reveal an Andersen much more human, fallible, and believable than before. Recent scholarship does not romanticize Andersen as an amiable, gentle if gawky, compassionate man of a high order of imagination. Recent Andersen scholarship has engaged in demythologizing this writer, in examining Andersen alongside the 19th century European cultural inspirations and revolutions, its social taboos and openings. For instance, noting social snobbery and social ambition as a recurrent theme in Andersen's tales, Alison Lurie delves into Andersen's psychological fluctuations and describes him as a vain, egotistic social climber suffering from "wild imagination, inner rage, tormenting anxieties and hypochondria, insatiable ambition" (9).

---

29 For instance: Lan Shouting, in his twice-published discussion on the tragic element in "The Little Mermaid", erroneously states that Andersen met and fell in love with Henriette Wulff before 1830 – before he met Riborg Voigt – and that Henriette and her brother Christian both died before 1830. Lan refers only to Andersen's autobiography translated/published in Chinese in 1983. Whether Lan's mistake is a result of mistranslation or misreading I do not know, as I do not return to this dated biography. However, my reading of recent Andersen biographies all state that it was in the 1850s the Wulff brother and sister passed away (the former in 1857, the latter in 1858); by then, Andersen, a man in his forties, had long since overcome his frustration over Riborg.

30 For instance, I find Johan de Mylius and Tiina Nunnally's biographical essay on Andersen to be delightfully succinct and lucid in dealing with the full range and scope of Andersen's life and career.

An explorer of artistic versatility and media, Andersen was interested in modern technology, industry and lifestyle. He travelled widely and much of the exotic sights and cultural ambiances he encountered are used to inform his writing. Anne-Marie Mai's essay brings Andersen outside the generic and textual confines of fairy tale, discussing Andersen and the 1867 World Exposition in Paris not only in relation to his less known story "The Dryad", but also in comparison with "The Little Mermaid". Likewise, Johs. Nørregaard Frandsen's discussion of Andersen as a cultural bridge-builder alerts us to the potential harm of treating Andersen exclusively as a writer for children. Also, Niels Ingwersen's review of recent four monographs on Andersen's writings shows that current scholarship has been exploring new perspectives and methodologies to enrich the world's understanding and appreciation of Andersen.[31] Johan de Mylius ("Our time") reminds us of a much-overlooked fact: by the time Andersen published his first small volume of fairy tales in 1835, he was already known in Danish literature "as a prolific author of poems, stage plays, and opera librettos" and travelogues – Andersen was "more of an author for adults, ironically hiding himself behind the mask of a children's author" and many of his tales yield a deeper sense if read not with a child's/child-like eye. On the other hand and from the new world, Jack Zipes observes that Andersen's fame in the English-speaking world does not rest solely on his fairy tales for children; instead, Andersen is appreciated for the diversity of his stories which vary considerably in length and style. For instance, as early as in 1985 Zipes studied "The Shadow" (1847) and categorized Andersen as "a significant precursor of surrealist and existentialist literature."

To advance Andersen studies in China we need to return Andersen to the contexts of literature and the arts, and accordingly accept, along with our exploration of reading and research, whatever possible human fallibility or proclivities Andersen may have exhibited or attempted to cloak. Andersen is a composite character in China: a writer of genius, a compassionate humanitarian, an acrid social humourist, and an allegorist of redemption. He is a self-made man, a naïve old fool,

---

31 Even if Andersen's later works are obscure and oblique, they can still shed light to his stylistic evolution and thematic range. For instance, having an English edition of *Schräge Märchen* helps, if we could not get it translated into Chinese directly. We can also learn about Denmark's/Europe's cultural history and aesthetic taste from the other types of writings by Andersen *even if* they are just mediocre.

a daft story-teller, a sad loser of unrequited love, an endearing doter on children. These images are partly created by the fabulist himself, partly inscribed to him by China's critics and readers. In China, the way Hans Christian Andersen is enthroned as a great writer for children and as *the* source of influence for China's children's literature has been a political move, part and parcel of the state's revolutionary project of modernization and hegemonic engineering. To date, three approaches are common in China's Andersen studies: biographical, humanist, and humanitarian. The biographical perspective links Andersen's life-story with his fairy tales, yielding a success case-study of a self-made man. The humanist perspective stems from the foci on Andersen's talent, his aesthetic artfulness, and the elevated, sublimated human emotions of his tales. The humanitarian perspective sees Andersen as a realist, a satirist, and a socialist with profuse empathy for the underclass. Zipes ("Critical Reflections") observes that as Andersen became popular with a religious, upper-class readership, his tales grew "conservative, cautious, and conventional." In his first few fairy tales, such as "The Tinderbox", "The Emperor's New Clothes", Andersen was indeed not afraid of poking fun at the ruling aristocracy and feudal monarchy; however, his tales would soon shed such provocative, dangerous undertones as they increasingly found an audience in Copenhagen's bourgeois homes and were obliged to replace such connotations by evangelical moralism or/and a servile attitude. This view is one big (stray?) step away from China's viewing Andersen as a socialist writer, a proletarian fighter. Calling Andersen "a failed revolutionary" will seriously upset the way China evaluates Andersen; how would current Chinese Andersen scholars take Zipes' controversial view that Andersen is "a man who hated to be dominated though he loved the dominant class"? (Zipes, "Discourse of the Dominated" 83).

What if Andersen is found to be *not* really a good fan of kids? Elias Bredsdorff devoted his career to "getting Andersen out of the nursery" because Andersen was always keenly aware that he was writing for adults as well as for children. Besides, addressing his tales to children was not without some strategic point, since it was a good way to get the educated Copenhagen middle-class adults – who, in Andersen's view, underappreciated him – to read along with their kids.

Also, what if Andersen is seen as a lesser talent? In the new light of recent research, Andersen may well become "imitative and eclectic": He did not "invent" the genre of fairy tale, though he did "revamp" the age-old genre of folktale and injected a lively, humorous personal touch into it (Zipes, "Discourse of the Dominated" 83-86).[32] Apart from Andersen's major contribution in using the language of common daily life to emphasize plain, colloquial accessibility, what strengths and faults are there in his other types of literary works? What can be learned from this about how an author battles against, or/and insinuates himself into, perceived cultural tastes and forms?

And, what if Andersen is found to be immodest and self-assertive? Research on Andersen's social networking reveals him to have actively courted fame and success. Uninvited, he often showed up at the doors of many important men-of-culture to introduce himself. Victor Hugo certainly was not the only person to be thus surprised (Frank 3). Moreover, what if we learn that Andersen – on his rise to fame in 1833 and with a royal stipend covering his travels abroad – had been inattentive to his dying mother: when she was suffering from and dying of alcoholism and poverty, she had sent him many letters pleading for help which he persistently ignored? (Tatar 381). What can be learned from this about the myth of self-fashioning, class and masculinity in 19th century Europe?

Andersen and Oscar Wilde were both introduced to China at the same time. While the former rapidly rose to the summit of distinction, the latter was soon to languish in relative oblivion. Why?[33] What if – just for one brief moment – Chinese critics and mature readers pause to examine Andersen's sexual frustration and anxieties, his desires towards the fair sex as well as the same sex, and accordingly re-read some of his tales in this light, as demonstrated by recent biographers and critics of Andersen?

All these *iffy* questions, if Andersen Studies in China as Children's Literature find them hard to swallow, is it any of Andersen's concern?[34]

---

32 Zipes notes that half of the nine fairy tales Andersen first published between 1835 and 1836 stem from tales already circulating in print and in the oral tradition.
33 Zhou Zuoren once discussed the respective merits of Andersen and Oscar Wilde with Zhao Jingshen (赵景深), famous translator of Andersen and professor of classical Chinese dramatic arts. Their correspondence of 1922 indicates that common consensus held Andersen to be superior to Wilde because "Andersen is closer to revealing children's nature" and "Wilde sometimes indulges in abstract, obscure thoughts such as wisdom, or love." (Wang Quangen *Andersen Research*, 23-25. My translation).
34 Obviously it *was* Andersen's concern when he was alive. This is what makes the cultural studies of his works so fascinating regarding 19th century European structures of feeling. Since Albert Hansen in 1901 brought up the issue of Andersen's sexuality, such inquiries have never been absent. However, it was not until the late 20th century that

What we gain from queering/querying Andersen and his literary works is a chance to historicize this writer, to contextualize him as a person, under the circumstances and structures of feeling of 19th century Europe. The point of such an inquiry is *not* to pin down Andersen's sexual orientation, but, I would argue, to find out what attitude towards sexuality, critical or common alike, our own cultures endorse or reject. It is not an iconoclastic rebellion, but a journey towards a fuller understanding of the past and our respective present, in the hope of building a less confusing/confused future. Andersen would be coyly smiling should he get to hear of this.

---

this issue became critically viable and valid (Frank 10). Yet, Andersen Studies in China have remained either blindly innocent of the latest research by Elias Bredsforff, Jackie Wullschlager, Jens Andersen, and Jack Zipes in this regard, or curiously reticent about this apocryphal revelation.

Hans Christian Andersen in China
An Overview

Ye Rulan
Lecturer, Research Fellow of the Nordic Literature Research Institute, Fudan University

> When he created a Chinese nightingale in one of his fairy tales, Hans Christian Andersen would never have imagined that he himself would become the "nightingale" singing in the dreams of 20th century Chinese children. – *China Daily*, 1 April, 2005

Hans Christian Andersen (1805-1875), the first Danish writer whose name was internationally recognized and whose works aroused global interest, was introduced into China in the early 20th century. After the arrival of his fairy tales, children's literature in China underwent a phase of drastic development.

The popularity of Hans Christian Andersen in China was very well demonstrated in various public opinion polls. A poll called "50 Books That Have Touched the Nation", undertaken in 1999, found Andersen ranking 7th, the only children's literature within the top ten (*Guangming Daily*,《光明日报》, 24 September, 1999). Another survey of "10 Greatest Books of the Millennium" in Hong Kong showed that *Fairytale Collection of Hans Christian Andersen* was 3rd on the list, right after the two great Chinese classics: *A Dream of Red Mansions* (《红楼梦》) and *The Pilgrimage to the West* (《西游记》) (*Chongqing Daily*,《重庆日报》, 21 December, 1999). *Fairytale Collection of Hans Christian Andersen* was also included in the recommendation list of "Ten Great Books for Children" made by People.com in 2010.[1] As Lars Seeberg – secretary-general of the Odense-based Hans Christian Andersen 2005 Foundation – has pointed out: "China is the country, if any, where the love of Andersen is perhaps almost as great as in his own country."

---

1 http://book.people.com.cn/GB/108221/11741440.html

The Introduction and Translation of Hans Christian Andersen in China

The first appearance of Hans Christian Andersen's name in China was in February 1909 in an article entitled "Review of Famous European and American Novels" written by the Chinese scholar Sun Yuxiu (孙毓修, 1871-1922).[2] In that article Sun briefly presented Andersen's life story and attributed the popularity of his stories to his colloquial and humorous writing style. As there was no such thing as a fairytale genre in China at the time, he defined Andersen's fairy tales as "adventure, spirit and monster stories (神怪小说)" (Sun Yuxiu, "Adventure, spirit…", "The Writer of adventure, spirit…"). Furthermore, the value of Andersen's fairy tales was not yet fully recognized then because in the eyes of the Chinese scholars his writings didn't touch upon the spirit of patriotism, or contain sharp admonitions to meet the needs of the social and cultural reform in China in the 1910s–1920s. Nevertheless, the fertile imagination in Andersen's fairy tales aroused the interest of a handful of readers. Less than a month later, Andersen's name appeared again in *A Collection of Foreign Stories* (《域外小说集》)[3] in the column "Herald of Forthcoming Books" (Zheng Jinhuai, "Who first introduced" 97) that informed readers of Andersen's fairy tales in the next issue.

Hans Christian Andersen's name was first translated by Zhou Zuoren into "安兑尔然 (An Dui-erran)" in two of his articles, namely "A Brief Remark on Fairy Tales" and "A Biography of the Danish Poet Hans Christian Andersen", and was later changed to the version that we use now, "安徒生 (An Tusheng)", which is much more in line with the pattern of traditional Chinese names, "An (安)" being the last name and "Tusheng (徒生)" being the first name. "安(An)" is a common Chinese surname recorded in *The Book of Hundred Family Names*[4]. "徒 (Tu)" literally means "apprentice" and "生 (Sheng)" means "born". When put together "徒生 (Tusheng)" generates the implication

---

2   Sun Yuxiu. (《读欧美名家小说札记》), 《东方杂志》, 1909年第6卷第1号"文苑"栏目.
3   It's a book of foreign short stories that are translated into Chinese by two Chinese writers and scholars Zhou Zuoren (周作人, 1885-1967) and Lu Xun (鲁迅, 1881-1936).
4   *The Book of Hundred Family Names* was compiled in the early northern Song Dynasty. It's a reference book of common Chinese family names. The number "hundred" in the book title means not exactly 100 family names, but "numerous". As a matter of fact, there are 438 family names altogether in the book. "An" ranks 110th.

of "born into a poor family", a vivid depiction of Andersen's family background.

The acceptance of Hans Christian Andersen's fairy tales has undergone several phases: budding in the early 1910s, blooming in the late 1910s, flourishing in the 1920s, hibernating from the 1930s to the 1940s, and branching out since the 1950s.

As China's New Culture Movement[5] spearheaded the development of children's literature in China, Zhou Zuoren – one of the great leaders in the New Culture Movement – endeavoured to establish the theoretical guiding principle for children's literature in China. The books of Nordic and Western literary criticism he happened to encounter in a second-hand bookstore in Tokyo reshaped and broadened his perspective in interpreting Andersen. When he realized the great potential value of Andersen's fairy tales for the development of Chinese children's literature, he couldn't wait to bring the stories to Chinese readers and explain to them the significance of Andersen's writing. In September 1913 Zhou Zuoren gave a brief introduction to Hans Christian Andersen in his article "A Brief Remark on Fairy Tales" (《童话略论》) published in the *Monthly Magazine of Ministry of Education Editorial Department*. In December 1913 he published another article entitled "The Biography of the Danish Poet Andersen" (《丹麦诗人安兑尔然传》) in *Ruo Club Periodical* (《乄社丛刊》) to further introduce the writer. It was the first in-depth introduction to Andersen in China. He commented that "Andersen's fairy tales observe the world through the eyes of children and represent it with a poetic touch. Such works are unprecedented, natural and beautiful." It was not long before Hans Christian Andersen became a hot topic in the literary world in China. In July 1914, Liu Bannong (刘半农, 1891-1934) published the first Chinese translation and rewriting of Andersen's "The Emperor's New Clothes" in a well-known Shanghai literature magazine *China Fiction World* (《中华小说界》). In 1917 Sun Yuxiu edited the first issue of *Fairy Tale* magazine and published his translation of "The Hardy Tin Soldier" and "The Little Mermaid". Another writer and translator Zhou

---

5   The New Culture Movement, also known as the "Chinese Renaissance" in the West, took place from the 1910s to the 1920s. Led by many new intellectuals who were well exposed to foreign civilisations, it was an intellectual revolution that sought to attack traditional Confucian concepts and traditional ethics, and usher in a new culture based on Western theories of democracy and science.

Shoujuan (周瘦鹃, 1895-1968) published his translation along with a portrait of Andersen, which gave the Chinese readers the opportunity to get a glimpse of Hans Christian Andersen's appearance (*A Collection of European Short Stories*).

With the rapid spread of Andersen's reputation, more and more writers got involved in translating and introducing Andersen's fairy tales. However, the conservative writers' adherence to orthodoxy snuffed the life and vitality out of the original versions. In 1918 Zhou Zuoren published a commentary in an influential monthly literary magazine *New Youth*,[6] in which he sharply criticized the awkward versions of "ancient Chinese literati" of Andersen's fairy tales by pointing out that the rigid use of archaic language style had "obliterated the childish interest and distorted the perspectives of children". In order to reverse that trend he published his translation of "The Little Match Girl" (1919) and "The Emperor's New Clothes" (1920) in the same magazine to further demonstrate his viewpoints. His comments and opinions soon gained attention from a broad range of readers and helped promote the national prevalence of Andersen's fairy tales.

Apart from the efforts of Zhou Zuoren, Zhao Jingshen (赵景深, 1902-1985), a writer and educator, finished the translation of 14 fairy tales in 1924 and had the book *Selected Fairy Tales of Andersen* published by New Culture Book Club, which was the very first published collection of a Chinese translation of Andersen's fairy tales.

Following Zhao's efforts, different translated versions kept springing up on mainland China. Gu Junzheng[7] (顾均正, 1902-1980) and Xu Tiaofu[8] (徐调孚, 1901-1981) stood out prominently with their translation of some of Andersen's fairy tales. Apart from translating, Gu Junzheng also wrote a book entitled *Hans Christian Andersen: A Biography* and had it published in 1928 by Shanghai Kaiming Book Store (上海开明书店). It is the first Hans Christian Andersen biography

---

6 *New Youth* (《新青年》), founded in 1915 in Shanghai, was the New Culture Movement's flagship magazine. It was a monthly magazine that aimed at advocating the thoughts of science and democracy, and new literary creations. It had a great impact throughout China during the New Culture Movement.

7 Gu Junzheng was a modern Chinese science writer, publisher, and translator. In 1926 he was invited to offer a course of World Fairy Tales at Shanghai University. Apart from literary creation and translation, he was also a main editor of *World Juvenile Literature Series* (《世界少年文学丛刊》).

8 The writer and translator Xu Tiaofu worked as an editor for *Literature Weekly* (《文学周报》) and *Fiction Monthly* from 1922 to 1932.

to be written by a Chinese writer. It's a pity that it was printed in small numbers and has never been reprinted. However, his contribution to introducing Andersen in China is well recognized.

In 1925 in celebration of the 120th anniversary of Andersen's birth, Zheng Zhenduo (郑振铎, 1898-1958), the editor of the first and most reputable and authoritative literature magazine in China, *Fiction Monthly*[9] (《小说月报》), released two "Andersen special issues" to offer readers an extensive introduction to Hans Christian Andersen and his literary creations. In the preamble he wrote that Andersen opened up a fantastic fairytale world with his childlike heart and poetic talent and referred to him as "the greatest writer of fairy tales in the world". The two issues included twenty-two translated stories, thirteen historical articles and literary reviews.

Zheng Zhenduo, together with Zhou Zuoren and several other writers, initiated the movement of children's literature in the 1920s and became the leading force in the early construction of children's literature in China. He made a comment on Hans Christian Andersen in *Literature Compendium* (《文学大纲》):[10] "Though he does not use ornate rhetoric, nor intentionally garnish or pick fancy phrases, his unadorned text, like a pure jade without any decoration, shines with glamorous and radiant splendour. His fairy tales are the best choice for children as well as the most favourable for adults. They are not just interesting stories, but the most beautiful poems written in prose." (Zheng Zhenduo, *Literature Compendium* 405-407). He also thought that Hans Christian Andersen's written words read as if they were uttered to the readers. "He told the stories to the children before he put pen to paper. It might well explain why Andersen's language is so authentic, tangible and cute." (Zheng Zhenduo, "Preface"). As a matter of fact, Andersen's language style is exactly what the Modern Vernacular Movement[11] tried to advocate. The introduction of Andersen's fairy tales undoubtedly provided a great model for

---

9 *Fiction Monthly* started publication in 1910 and has had the largest circulation in China.
10 First published in the 1920s, Zheng Zhenduo's *Literature Compendium* is a great work of world literature. The book ranges from the beginning of human civilisation to the early 20th century and includes literary giants and their works, both ancient and modern, Chinese and foreign.
11 The Modern Vernacular Movement was considered to be a crucial part of the New Culture Movement. It was launched by a group of intellectuals who had received Western education around 1919. They advocated the substitution of ancient Chinese by the modern Chinese language. It was considered a positive result of the emancipation of the mind.

its advocators and, to a certain extent, helped the movement to become victorious. Zhou Zuoren's contribution to the introduction and translation of Andersen is that he systematically introduced Hans Christian Andersen to Chinese readers, and was the first to encourage the use of modern Chinese vernacular in the translations, while the great contribution of Zheng Zhenduo is that he promoted the massive dissemination that brought Andersen's fairy tales into almost every Chinese family.

During the 1930s and 1940s, children's literature from the Soviet Union poured into China and almost drowned out Hans Christian Andersen's voice. The fervent passion for Andersen's fairy tales among scholars at the 120th anniversary of Andersen's birth failed to recur after a decade. Although the translation work continued and the statistics show that from the 1930s to the founding of the People's Republic of China in 1949, approximately 25 versions of Andersen's Fairy Tale Collections (Li Hongye, *Chinese Interpretations* 110) appeared, the world of Andersen went into hibernation. Zhou Zuoren published four Andersen's fairy tales in *National News Weekly* in 1936, but there was scarcely any response (Li Hongye, *Chinese Interpretations* 122).

The Andersen wave returned in the 1950s and the number of the translations increased enormously. Among the Chinese translators devoted to the translation of the complete collection of Andersen's fairy tales, Ye Junjian (叶君健, 1914-1999), Ren Rongrong (任溶溶 1923-), Lin Hua (林桦 1927-2005) and Shi Qin'e (石琴娥 1936-) were the most outstanding. They greatly enriched the library of translated works of Andersen and provided the readers with the chance to savour his fairy tales with different flavours of translation. Each rendering has its distinctive features. As Ye Junjian remarked in the preface of *A Complete Hans Christian Andersen* (《安徒生童话全集》), "Over the century, the beautiful fairy tales have been going around from perennially snow-covered Iceland to the blazing Equator. They have been published in various languages with numerous varieties of copies." (Ye Junjian, "Preface").

Ye Junjian was the first to translate the complete fairy tales of Hans Christian Andersen. Having read Andersen's original works in England in 1944, he published his first book of translations in 1953 and kept working on the subsequent volumes. He is known as the first Chinese to translate Hans Christian Andersen directly from Danish. His four-volume book *The Complete Hans Christian Andersen Fairy Tales* was published in 1978 and has been considered the most authoritative translation in China. In the preface of the book, he interpreted Andersen's fairy tales as a mix of imaginative stories, political satire and poetic language, permeated with romanticism and humanitarianism. In the translation he tried to retain the poetic touch, the expressive language, and the smart humour of the original works and bring out Hans Christian Andersen not only as a storyteller, but as a great writer and poet. In 1999 he re-translated Andersen's fairy tales into *A Complete Hans Christian Andersen*, referring not only to the original Danish version, but the English version published by Oxford University Press and his own published translations. The book, which comprised 164 fairy tales with annotations and his brief commentary attached to each, further replenished the world of Andersen in China. Queen Margrethe II of Denmark awarded Ye Junjian the Order of the Dannebrog for his great contribution. His translation, considered as "faithful, expressive and elegant", has always been taken as a translation at "the highest level".

Lin Hua's working experience as a diplomat in the Chinese Embassy in the Kingdom of Denmark gave him many opportunities to get a first-hand feel and access to the materials of Hans Christian Andersen. On 2 April, 1955, he found the germ of the idea to study and translate Andersen when he attended the spectacular celebration in Odense of the 150th anniversary of Andersen's birth as the interpreter for the Chinese Embassy, but he didn't set out the task of translation from Danish to Chinese until he retired in 1988. Before his translation of *The Complete Works of Andersen's Fairy Tales* – a collection of 157 fairy tales – came out in 1994, he was mainly engaged in research work on Hans Christian Andersen. He felt that the focus on fairy tales resulted in an ignorance of Andersen's achievements in other literary and artistic fields, such as the novel, poetry, prose, drama, papercuts and painting. At a ceremony in commemoration of Andersen's bicentenary in Copenhagen, Lin Hua expressed his hope that "the different new renditions of Andersen's works created on the bicentenary celebration of his birth can broaden the Chinese readers' perspectives of Andersen's literary achievements and make them better acquainted with Danish culture and history" (*China Daily*, 1 April, 2005). His translation of *Collected Works of Andersen* (《安徒生文集》), which includes Andersen's fairy tales, novels, poetry, dramas, and essays, brings to the readers a much more complete Hans Christian Andersen. In addition, Lin Hua shared with the readers more than ten of Andersen's sketches, each with his comments in *A Picture Book without Pictures* (2004); and introduced Andersen's papercuts in another book entitled *Impressions on Hans Christian Andersen's Paper-cutting* (《安徒生剪影》) published in 2005.

Among the Chinese translators of Andersen's fairy tales, Ren Rongrong is also renowned as a great writer for children. His translation of Hans Christian Andersen from English gave prominence to the vivid, humorous and beautiful language style that accommodates to children's taste. He used simple language and oral expressions so that the stories are as if told directly to the readers. Shi Qin'e translated Andersen directly from Danish and her efforts brought out the original flavour of the fairy tales. On 1 June, 2012, she published the Collector's Edition of *Hans Christian Andersen's Fairy Tales*.

Up to now, there are more than 10 versions of *The Complete Works of Fairy Tales by Hans Christian Andersen*, and approximately 200 different translations of selected fairy tales. After a century of international cultural exchange, Andersen's fairy tales have now become a classic in the library of Chinese children's literature and continue to be influential and popular.

Andersen's Influence in China

The impact of Andersen in China can be traced back to as early as the May Fourth New Culture Movement. Before Andersen's fairy tales were introduced, students who had studied abroad during the late Qing Dynasty had brought back a handful of foreign children's literature such as *Aesop's Fables, Cuore, Robinson Crusoe,* and Jules Verne's science fiction, providing rich spiritual nourishment to children of the time. But in the context of social changes, people were more concerned about works that were conducive to ideological and political education. The outburst of the New Culture Movement changed the situation. It promoted a demotic consciousness of democracy and aroused people's awareness of equality and freedom. Women, children and farmers, who had been regarded as subordinate in the feudal patriarchal society, were extracted from their unfair predicament. Children's image in the adult world was no longer that of mini-adults but of individuals with a distinct, independent existence. Their rights and specific needs, and how their education would determine the future of the whole nation began to be taken seriously by modern scholars and educators (Li Hongye *Chinese Interpretations*, 86-93).

Among the revolutionists, Zhou Zuoren was far ahead of his contemporaries in realizing the significance of children's education and initiating the children's literature movement. He realized that Andersen's fairy tales would blaze a trail for the traditional intellectuals who were still imprisoned in the old stereotypes. Compared with the serious classical reading materials for children, Andersen's fairy tales were like a breath of fresh air to Chinese children, and like fresh blood that would renew their life. The spread of Hans Christian Andersen's fairy tales in China ushered in the process of modernization of Chinese children's literature and nurtured a group of writers of children's literature. "Foreign fairy tales, especially the ones written by Hans Christian Andersen, are a wonderful inspiration and influence to Chinese children's literature and promoted the establishment of a team specializing in the creation of fairy tales for Chinese children." (Wang Quangen 111). Gu Junzheng expressed in "Hans Christian Andersen: A Biography": "Andersen's fairy tales have aroused our greatest interest in children's literature, and therefore our determination to be engaged in this career is intensified." Zhao Jingshen commented that "there are two important things about Andersen: (1) children-friendliness: Every element of his fairy tales takes account of the children's mental world. (2) a mirror of natural beauty: His fairy tales are suffused with a poetic touch." What has impressed the Chinese writers most in Andersen's fairy tales, is the outstanding characteristics of the child. As Ye Shengtao (叶圣陶 1894-1988[12]) pointed out: "In the 1920s people were deeply impressed by the 'poetic style', 'the spirit of children', 'childlike language' and 'wild thoughts' as they read Andersen's fairy tales." (Li Hongye *Chinese Interpretations*, 118-119). The free, causal style of expression corresponds perfectly to children's mode of perception.

The years of wars during the 1930s and 40s in China pushed Andersen aside, for people were taken up with more practical concerns. Andersen's fairy tales were thought of as "escapism", void of realistic significance. Fortunately, this trend of thought didn't last long. Through the efforts of modern writers and translators, Andersen's

---

12 Ye Shengtao was a renowned Chinese writer, educator, and publisher. He was one of the founders of the first Association for Literary Studies (文学研究会) during the May Fourth Movement in China. His motto "Literature is for life" enjoyed wide currency.

fame in China was regained in the 1950s. More importantly, Andersen's fairy tales are thought of as not only written for children but for the adult world as well. Chinese readers have realized that Andersen's fairy tales "win the heart of children with his language style" and "gain wide acceptance among adults with his profundity" (Zhao Lingli). Andersen's fairy tales are considered as the most distinguished model for children's literature as they are "the children's favourite adult's literature, and the adults' favourite children's literature." (Zhao Lingli). Zhang Xiaofeng (张晓风, 1941-), a famous essayist in Taiwan, wrote a verse entitled "The Intimate Topic From the Age of 5 to 55" to express the powerful influence of Hans Christian Andersen's works to people of all ages:

> *If a 5-year-old kid has not yet listened to Andersen,*
> *his childhood will not be warm enough;*
> *If a 15-year-old juvenile has not yet read Andersen,*
> *his adolescence will not be colourful enough;*
> *If a 25-year-old youth has not yet savoured Andersen,*
> *his adulthood will not be brilliant enough;*
> *If a 35-year-old man has not yet learned Andersen,*
> *the summer of his life will not be rich enough;*
> *If a 45-year-old man has not yet pondered Andersen,*
> *the autumn of his life will not be profound enough;*
> *If a 55-year-old man has not yet reviewed Andersen,*
> *his twilight years will not be leisurely enough.*

Andersen's fairy tales inspired a number of Chinese writers to become writers of children's literature. Ye Shengtao is an early such practitioner. *The Scarecrow* – his collection of 23 fairy tales written during 1921 and 1922 – was the first book of Chinese fairy tales. From 1929 to 1930 he finished writing his second book of fairy tales *An Ancient Hero's Statue*. In 1930 he created a sequel to "the Emperor's New Clothes". The following is an extract of his version:

> Derided by the public in the procession, the naked emperor flew into a rage out of humiliation and announced: "Whoever says bad things about me will be executed immediately!" As soon as the command was given, fifty people lost their lives on the spot. Since then, the emperor no longer wore other clothes.

One day when his favourite concubine was drinking with him, she said inadvertently: "Oh, Your Majesty, the wine stained your chest!" With that slip of the tongue, she was banished to the cold palace. On another occasion, a minister said after his resignation: "Fortunately, I no longer need to face the naked emperor." What he got in return was death as he was found guilty of defying the emperor's ban.

Once the emperor was patrolling the capital, and wherever he went his ears were so filled with joking from his people that he was driven to an extreme act of violence. More than a thousand innocent people were killed.

A compassionate old minister thought of a way to change this situation. He went to the emperor and said: "Your Majesty, you have always liked new clothes. What about ordering a new suit?" But the emperor insisted that the magic clothes he was wearing would never be worn out and threw the minister into prison. The people requested for "freedom of speech and freedom of laughing and joking" only to be rejected by the emperor.

Henceforward, everyone tried to avoid the emperor. But the emperor was still suspicious. He ordered his soldiers to search from house to house, arrest anyone who laughed at home and punish them by death. His tyranny sparked the revolt of the people. They flocked together, besieged the emperor, tore his flesh, and shouted: "Rip off your non-existent clothes!" Finally, even the soldiers stood on the side of the people. The emperor, as if hit in the head by a big rock falling from the sky, collapsed on the ground. As the emperor was overthrown, people elected that innocent child, who was believed to bring them benefits, to sit on the throne.

Though Ye Shengtao set out to write fairy tales under the influence of Andersen, it's quite obvious that his style is very different from Andersen's. His writing is more realistic and critical. He did create some stories about "beauty" and "love" such as "The Little White Boat" and "The Swallow", which echoes the theme of Andersen's "The Little Mermaid", "The Wild Swans", and "Thumbelina", however, most of Ye Shengtao's stories are presentations of his reflection on the complex social changes and conflicts between classes in that era.

The 1940s witnessed the rise of another writer of fairy tales, Yan Wenjing (严文井, 1915-2005). Compared with Ye Shengtao's works, his writing is more strongly influenced by Andersen in terms of the style of language, the use of images, and the poetic style. "Singer Boy (《歌孩》)", for example, uses the same image of "moon" as *A Picture Book without Pictures* (*Billedbog uden Billeder*, 1839) by Andersen. Yan

Wenjing also mimics the structure of that story and starts his fairy tale with "The moon told me a story…" (Li Hongye, *Chinese Interpretations* 157-158). In the postscript of his first book of fairy tales, *Nannan and the Beard Uncle* (《南南和胡子伯伯》, 1941), he writes: "I got to know Andersen in my youth. [...] He stands higher than any other writer of fairy tales. What he guides people to experience is not just a fantastic world. His stories lead us to something that we are familiar with in our life, but not within reach. He's like a magician, capable of endowing anything with radiance with his magic wand… I have felt the power of literature from his fairy tales, and it occurs to me that I might write something too." (323).

The spread of Andersen's fairy tales has gone on unabated even till now because what he described in the stories is universal human nature. For instance, "The Emperor's New Clothes" is a timeless story because "it brings us to the everlasting topic – human weakness." "The Emperor and the officers in the story are not only stupid and ridiculous, but poor and pitiable as well. As we, the readers, laugh over the absurdity of the characters, we may just realize how close we are to the poor characters. It resonates with people of different ages, different nations and different races." (Pan Yang).

Cao Wenxuan, one of the most remarkable contemporary writers of children's literature, expresses the same pursuit as Andersen, i.e. the beauty and profundity of literature. He strongly recommends Hans Christian Andersen to his readers by saying: "If anyone hopes to elevate himself, he should read Andersen. If anyone wants to develop better taste, he should also read Andersen." (44-45). Another contemporary children's literature writer, Yang Hongying (杨红樱, 1962-), regards Andersen as her first teacher of creative writing, and her understanding of love has been shaped by Andersen's "The Little Mermaid" which, according to her interpretation, is about sacrifice and nobility of mind. Her first encounter with Andersen's books can be traced back to the age of seven, and she is still reading them because she thinks that the stories taste differently for people of various ages. "The meaning of stories such as 'The Emperor's New Clothes' is renewed with each reading. Although what children can get out of the fairy tales is different from what adults do, they are perfectly able to understand Andersen."[13]

---

13 http://news.sina.com.cn/o/2005-03-27/02365473112s.shtml

The New Generation writers have also been nurtured by Andersen's stories. Guo Jingming (郭敬明, 1983-), a noted representative of post-1980s writers, said in an interview in 2011: "Hans Christian Andersen's tragic beauty has had a very great influence on my writing. His fairy tales, instead of being lighthearted and happy, are exceptionally cruel. His words are as cold and desolate as the moonlight. 'The Little Mermaid', 'The Snow Queen' and 'The Little Matchstick Girl' are about tragic beauty."[14]

Hans Christian Andersen's fairy tales have continued to influence China because his stories are considered as a life-long companion for Chinese readers. A contemporary writer, Bi Shumin (毕淑敏, 1952-), noted down her changing perceptions of "The Little Mermaid" at different ages in "The Constantly Renewed Little Mermaid":

> When I read the fairy tale for the first time at the age of eight, I couldn't help crying and crying because I felt it too tragic for the beautiful princess to melt into bubbles in the sea. I didn't notice the element of love. I was most worried when she became dumb, and I thought of her dumbness as the root of her tragedy.
>
> When I read it at 18, I perceived love in the story. The little mermaid was willing to sacrifice herself for her true love. How respectable! How unselfish!
>
> When I became a mom and read it again at 28, I was more concerned about the family bond in the story. When the little mermaid was in trouble, the old queen, regardless of the state of her health, rose above the sea to care for her granddaughter. I was deeply touched by the old granny's benevolence.
>
> When I became a writer and turned to it again at 38, I started to focus more on Andersen's writing techniques. I tried to imagine how he wrote, and how he designed the ending of the story. I also wondered if Andersen was satisfied with this ending. Is it too heavy for children? (Li Hongye, *Chinese Interpretations* 316-319)

Some may ask "Will Andersen continue to survive in the contemporary world? Do his works meet the needs of the new era? Do his stories adapt to the tastes of the contemporary people?" The children born after the 90s turn out to be less familiar with Andersen's works

---

14 http://www.cnwest88.com/2011/rwzx_1008/91378.html

because the open world enables them to have access to all forms of children's literary art from different countries. But the positive thing is that efforts to share the spirit of Hans Christian Andersen have never stopped.

The Dissemination and Rewriting of Andersen in China

With textbooks, translated works of Andersen, cultural activities, stage performances, and commercial projects, the dissemination of Andersen's works is fairly diversified and very active in China.

"The Pea Blossom", "The Ugly Duckling", "The Emperor's New Clothes", "The Little Matchstick Girl", and "The Little Mermaid" are included in primary and secondary school textbooks. Normally the curriculum includes a teacher's introduction to Andersen's life story and his papercuts, and a discussion by the students of what underlies the stories. Apart from the textbooks, students can refer to a good number of *Hans Christian Andersen's Fairy Tales* available in bookstores. They are reprinted every year for the constant needs of readers.

Cultural activities are an important booster for Andersen's dissemination. On the International Children's Day in 2005, the State Post Bureau issued a set of five special stamps of Andersen's fairy tales – the Emperor's New Clothes, the Little Mermaid, Thumbelina, the Little Match Girl, the Ugly Duckling – to celebrate the bicentenary of Andersen's birth. At the same time, Hong Kong Post Bureau also launched a set of stamps with four pieces designed with traditional Chinese papercuts. "The Ugly Duckling", "The Emperor's New Clothes", "The Little Matchstick Girl", and "The Little Mermaid" are "cut" onto the stamps, linking Andersen closer to Chinese readers.

On June 1, 2012, a new set of four Andersen fairy tale stamps, together with folders, first day covers (FDC) and special souvenir sheets, were globally issued. Chinese designs were adopted for the Andersen stamps. The stories of "The Wild Swans", "The Nightingale", "The Shepherdess and the Chimney-Sweeper", "What the Old Man Does Is Always Right" have been drawn in the Piyingxi (皮影戏, Chinese shadow puppetry art[15]) style by the Chinese designer Shen Jiahong

---

15 Shadow puppets are flat articulated figures cut from leather. In the shadow show, the cut-out figures are held between a source of light and a translucent screen. The plays are performed by moving the puppets and light source behind the screen.

and engraved on blocks for printing by the Norwegian engraver Martin Mörck. In addition, the stamps have integrated image recognition technology which enables smartphones to recognize the pictures on the stamps and receive relevant animations. Each story stamp has a corresponding FDC which includes a story sketch card inside. The special souvenir sheets highlight the Danish fairy tales with the original Chinese papercuts. The blending of the Chinese art form and Andersen's fairy tales help promote the penetration and localisation of Hans Christian Andersen in China.

Andersen's fairy tales have always been regarded as a master copy for diversified representation and a rich nutrient for new creations. The adaptation of Andersen's fairy tales into stage plays, and multimedia arts has been very fruitful in China.

In 1955 "The Emperor's New Clothes" was made into a radio play by Zhang Qingren (张庆仁, 1924-), a well-known radio playwright of the China Central Broadcasting Station. On the day of the 150th anniversary of Hans Christian Andersen's birth, the play was broadcast during the News Report Programme, which was unprecedented and won rave reviews.

In 1992, Ju Ping (鞠萍, 1966-) – CCTV's famous children's show host and Ambassador of Goodwill in China for the 200th anniversary of Andersen's birth – performed a recital of Ye Junjian's translation of *A Complete Hans Christian Andersen* and recorded it onto tapes when she was pregnant. She did so because she felt that Andersen's stories are the best for unborn babies, since they can mould a myriad of babies into angels. In 2010 her recordings were converted into 40 CDs and re-edited into four volumes (Self-improvement, Wisdom of Life, Heart-warming Stories, and Adventures).

In 1978 the first Chinese ballet adaptation of "The Little Match Girl" was made under the guidance of Ye Junjian. The famous composer Huang Anlun (黄安伦, 1949-) was invited to write the music for the ballet performance. In 2005 this ballet was rehearsed in Beijing Academy of Dance by the students and brought back onto the stage in Beijing.[16] The prototype of the little match girl in Andersen's fairy tales was transplanted onto the stage in China and was re-set against the backdrop of the Chinese society, with her articulating her despair and hopes in that specific social context.

---

16 http://ent.sina.com.cn/h/2005-12-19/1022933331.html

Xi'an Children's Art Theatre produced a pantomime of "The Ugly Duckling" in 1984. By 1999, the number of performance had reached over 1,500 (*Theatre and Opera in China*). Zhejiang Drama Art Academy created a new version of the play in 2012, with the opening performance in Hangzhou on Children's Day. The grand interactive puppet show invites the young audience to join in the performance and help the ugly duckling to change its fate. The interactive performance lets the audience feel as if they were participating in the development of the plot.

In 2002, Hebei Beijing Opera Theatre (河北省京剧院) mixed the traditional Chinese art form with Andersen's story and created a Beijing Opera pantomime of "The Wild Swans", with nationwide performances in 2003 (*Beijing Opera.* 2003: 3). This is an audacious attempt to blend traditional Chinese performing art with Andersen's fairy tales. The success of the performance further testifies that Andersen's fairy tales are global and all-embracing, not only in content but in spirit. In addition, Shanghai Puppet Theatre adapted "The Little Match Girl" into a puppet show and it has been performed since 2002.

In 2007, Chen Xinyi (陈薪伊, 1938-), a director at national level, wrote a play called *Andersen* and turned it into a big stage performance for children after her three years of research in Denmark. She made Andersen the protagonist and had him walk out of the picture frame and stand in front of the audience. The play showed Andersen's life journey from the son of a poor shoemaker to a world-famous writer, with the classical fairy tale characters such as the ugly duckling and the little mermaid either acting as bystanders or being part of Andersen's imaginary world, a perfect mixture of fantasy and reality that shortens the distance between the Danish writer and Chinese readers and gets the audience more involved in the intriguing and creative plot.

On April 7, 2007 after the advertising campaign of *Andersen*, Beijing Seven-Color-Light Children Theatre in Ju'er Hutong was chosen as Andersen's "home" in Beijing and had its name officially changed to Andersen Theatre, where Andersen's fairy tales would be staged at regular intervals. The play *Andersen* was co-produced by six major art theatres across China and a 500-member troupe was soon established for this performance in the new Andersen Theatre (*Beijing Daily*, 《北京日报》, 9 April, 2007). Less than two months later, *Andersen* made a successful debut in Beijing on Children's Day and was performed

30 times from June 1st to 3rd. The "*Andersen*" troupe put the play on again in 2009 in Shenyang and it has continued to prove popular.

Another modern drama *The Andersen Code* was staged from 30 September till 2 October, 2012, in Shanghai. It's an adventurous children's play co-produced by Shanghai Qixian Film and TV Culture Media Company and Beijing Big Cat Visual Studio. The play features a story of a little girl who, on coming across a black cat that can speak our human language, wanders accidently into a mysterious fairytale world. Pu Cunxin, acting as narrator in the performance, describes the upcoming play as "engrossing, joyful, novel and interesting". Wei Yang, the playwright, has explained that the play has been created to pay tribute to the great masters of fairy tales and the protagonist Xiao Duo is the embodiment of every child that has a deep love for the fairytale world.

Apart from being the preferred choice for stage performances, Andersen is now also hot on the Internet. Baidu Tieba[17] affiliated to Baidu.com, China's largest online communication platform designed by China's biggest search engine Baidu.com, established a discussion group called Andersen Bar in 2005, where people can ask questions about Hans Christian Andersen and his works, leave messages, write comments, share reading experiences, post pictures, cast votes and practise creative writing projects about Andersen.

The platform also provides a list of relevant links such as Fairy Tale Bar, Ye Junjian Bar, Grimm's Fairy Tale Bar, etc. By the end of September 2012, there had been 1,490 topics and 15,599 posts in Andersen Bar and they are updated on a daily basis.

Hans Christian Andersen as an international brand has also become established in China. DK H. C. ANDERSEN International Children's Products China Co., Ltd. was registered in Shanghai in 2005. Its headquarters are located at the Bund in Shanghai, and the business has since expanded to the Zhejiang, Guangzhou and Hubei provinces. In cooperation with DK H. C. Andersen Cultural Foundation, all kinds of Andersen-related industries have emerged[18]. Shanghai Andersen Cultural Hotel located at the Bund incorporated Andersen's fairy tales and papercuts in its layout. A little mermaid sculpture has been placed at the centre of the hotel lobby to highlight the featuring of the hotel brand.

---

17 http://tieba.baidu.com/f?kw=%B0%B2%CD%BD%C9%FA. Tieba – the Chinese phonetic transcripttion – means Paste Bar literally. Baidu Tieba was established in 2003.
18 http://www.hcadk.com/cn/index-cn.htm

Moreover, Andersen and his fairy tales have also permeated into China's entertainment industry. Located at New Jiangwan Town[19] (No. 200 Guohong Road) and covering an area of 81,400 square metres, Shanghai Andersen Children's Cultural Park integrates 18 fairy tales such as "The Little Mermaid", "The Ugly Duckling", "Thumbelina", and "The Emperor's New Clothes", with the landscape. The project plan was made in 2006 and construction began in 2009. So far, the surrounding area has been basically completed and the interior will now be built into 18 European-style and distinctive scenes. The scheme also includes a Sculpture Square for the replica of the bronze statue of Hans Christian Andersen in the Royal Gardens in Copenhagen.[20]

The whole park will be divided into four units: (1) Andersen Castle, in which fairy tales are retold and reproduced using high-tech, (2) Science and Technology Museum, where children can start a journey into the "future world" with the aid of the cutting-edge technologies, (3) Theatre Zone, where children can participate in various hands-on activities such as writing and acting, (4) a shopping area, where Danish children's products are to be sold. As the first story-themed children's park on mainland China, Andersen Children's Cultural Park creates a world that combines education with recreation (*Youth Daily*,《青年报》, 14 May, 2009). The construction of the park has gained broad attention and high recognition as people keep expressing their wish to visit the place as soon as it is open to the public.

Cultural Mix – the Sustainable Development of Andersen in China

During Hans Christian Andersen's hundred-year's stay in China, the impact of his fairy tales has been enormous as his stories penetrate Chinese readers to the heart. His personal charm was fully revealed

---

19 Started in 2001, the urban planning of Shanghai New Jiangwan Town has made full use of the local natural resources and has successfully created the first eco-town in Shanghai. The town integrates modern residential areas with comprehensive community services, first-rate universities and school, libraries, advanced entertainment and sports facilities such as Andersen Children's Cultural Park, Wetland Park, yacht harbour and SMP Skate Park, which is the biggest Skate Park in the world, as well as convenient transportation systems.

20 In October 2008, Chairman of the Danish Cultural Institute Eric Messerschmidt authorized Shanghai Andersen Children's Cultural Park to replicate the bronze statue of Hans Christian Andersen in Copenhagen.

as his artistic talents were recognized. Each fairy tale sprang from the scissors of Hans Christian Andersen and the papercuts embodied the themes. A stronger link was thus established between Andersen and China. The folk art of paper cutting, which emerged in China as early as the Han Dynasty (206 BC–221 AD), resonated with the people. What makes the Andersen stories about papercuts more intriguing is their concision and ubiquity. The mix of the storytelling with the Chinese folk art has generated vivid tales that cut through time and space.

In the 21st century, the dynamism of Hans Christian Andersen in China remains undiminished, as his fairy tales have great potential for cultural mix. The stories are ideal prototypes for new literary and artistic creations. For the Chinese, Andersen is a fountain of infinite inspirations where everyone can find value. The rewriting and recreation of Andersen's fairy tales have boosted the prosperity of the Chinese artistic and cultural industry and, at the same time, they have instilled new life and energy into Andersen's world.

When Heritage Tourism goes Glocal
The Little Mermaid in Shanghai

Anne Klara Bom
PhD, the Hans Christian Andersen Center,
University of Southern Denmark

> The Little Mermaid is a very old cultural icon, but in our age it is becoming a symbol. By moving it from its original location and by changing its cultural surroundings questions of how we think about our cultural heritage and historical values are raised. (Ai Weiwei, Chinese artist. Ritzaus Bureau)

Heritage tourism is a branch of tourism in which tourists visit cultural heritage locations all over the world. To perform heritage tourism, it is thus presupposed that tourists travel and visit the actual heritage locations. When the World Exposition 2010 (Expo 2010) was held in Shanghai, China, from 1 May to 31 October, however, the Danish pavilion contained an important representative of the Danish cultural heritage, as the original statue of the Little Mermaid was physically transported from Denmark and placed in the middle of a basin in the pavilion. This moving of the Little Mermaid caused the population in Denmark to engage in a media debate, and the content of this debate is the topic of interest in this paper.[1]

Almost 200 countries were represented at Expo 2010 in Shanghai. Each country constructed a national pavilion at the exposition with its own interpretations of its nation and culture. The main attraction in the Danish pavilion was the statue of the Little Mermaid. During its six-month-long exile in Shanghai, 5.6 million people visited the Little Mermaid, and it was estimated that approximately 80-90% of the visitors were Chinese (Andersen, C.A.). The Danish pavilion had more visitors than those of other Scandinavian countries, and it is

---

1 This paper was originally published in *Journal of Heritage Tourism* (Vol. 7, No. 4, 2012) and it is reprinted in this book by permission of the publisher, Taylor & Francis Ltd.

likely that the reason for this was the Little Mermaid, as Hans Christian Andersen, who wrote the fairy tale about her, has considerable cultural significance in China.

The statue is one of the most visited tourist attractions in Denmark, and illustrations of it have been deployed to brand Denmark on several occasions. For Danes, the significance of the Little Mermaid is that it is part of their cultural heritage and that it belongs to Denmark, where it is located on a rock in Copenhagen Harbour. But when the Little Mermaid was relocated to the Danish pavilion in Shanghai, a new "present-day use of the past" (Ashworth; Graham, Ashworth and Tunbridge) was performed. Thus, the Little Mermaid's sojourn in China can be seen as a manifest example of a global-local fusion. When the statue was moved from its original location to the Shanghai Exposition, an item of local cultural heritage was moved to a field of global interest. This new way of using "the past as a resource for today" (Timothy and Boyd 12) can be perceived as *glocal heritage tourism*, as the local, represented by an iconic sculpture, and the global, represented by the Chinese people visiting the Danish pavilion, were brought together in a new constellation at the exposition.

In accordance with Robertson's sense of the concept of glocal, the local and the global levels are engaged in a dialectic relationship based on reciprocal constitution, as globalization has resulted in "the reconstruction, in a sense production, of 'home', 'community' and 'locality'" (30). The central aim of this paper is to clarify how glocalization in practice was perceived at the local level. It is offered as a thesis that this glocal perspective can contribute to a new way of thinking about and performing heritage tourism. The present scholarly focus within this field is primarily on the supply side of heritage tourism, covering, for example, "motivations and segmenting visitor markets" (Poria, Butler and Airey). This focus integrates the physical place of heritage as an important part of research. But for six months in 2010 at the Little Mermaid's original spot in Copenhagen Harbour, there was to be seen only a screen showing a live transmission of the statue in Shanghai. In order to analyse how representatives from the Danish population made sense of their cultural heritage and how this sense-making related to physical places, this paper integrates discussions from museology and anthropology, as the two fields have contributed with relevant insights into what is at stake when heritage artifacts cross borders.

Heritage Out of Place

While discussions about heritage out of place are scarce within tourism studies, the field of museology has presented extensive research concerned with this subject. Cultural heritage is exhibited every day in museums around the world, and it is common to exchange objects and exhibitions across borders. Scholars who have studied such exchanges have especially been concerned with the context of exhibitions, for example, the particular ideologies every culture is affected by when it collects and exhibits its own artifacts as well as objects from other cultures (Barringer; Pieterse; Vergo). These varied studies have in common a perception of the very act of collecting, exhibiting and moving of tangible culture as occurring within a discursive frame that reflects the hegemonic discourses in the exhibiting culture. For instance, Barringer's study of the exhibitions at the South Kensington Museum is simultaneously a study of how in the nineteenth century British, imperialistic identity was displayed in the different exhibitions. Barringer states that the "meaning of an object is inflected, even reinvented by the context in which it is displayed" (11-12).

In the case of the South Kensington Museum, the colonial context of the cultural artifacts was not integrated in the exhibition strategy. The opposite was the case with the exhibition Te Maori in the 1980s. Te Maori was an exhibition of cultural artifacts from the Maori culture organized by New Zealand Museums and Maori groups in cooperation with the Metropolitan Museum of Art in New York (Brown). The Maori people term their tangible and intangible cultural heritage *taonga* and they believe that taonga contains representations of their ancestors. Thus, the symbolic value of taonga is of great importance to them, and Te Maori was the first exhibition of taonga realized with the consent and cooperation of the Maori people: when the taonga was moved from New Zealand to New York, representatives from the Maori people even accompanied the exhibition as caretakers (Moko Mead). The Metropolitan redefined the Maori objects as art, and Brown sees this redefinition as a demonstration of how the "Maori material culture, disciplined by museum display, could be associated with modernity, sophistication and market values" (Brown 290). The Maori people were thrilled by this recontextualization of their cultural heritage and perceived the exhibition as a reason for national pride (290). A reason for this satisfaction can be that the narrative attached to Te Maori integrated the symbolic value attached to taonga by the Maori people instead of superseding it.

These two cases can be seen as examples of glocal heritage tourism, as they contain two different kinds of a global-local fusion. The course of events in the exhibitions indicates at least two important aspects that will be taken into account in the following examination of how the Danish population made sense of the loan of the Little Mermaid. First, the examples show that the meaning and value attached to the heritage in question by the local and global representatives have pivotal status in an examination of heritage glocalization in practice. Second, the examples indicate that these meanings and values change when the cultural heritage is displaced.

Banal Nationalism and Property Language

This present-day use of the Little Mermaid in Shanghai activated the Danish commentators' sense of national identity. In analyses of national identity in practice, social psychologist Michael Billig has introduced the notion of banal nationalism (Billig, *Talking*; *Banal*; "Discursive"), covering the "routine ways" in which "citizens of the state are reminded that they live in a nation within a world of nation-states" (Billig, "Discursive" 219). Billig illustrates his point with the example of the nation flag:

> [...] the citizen of the nation-state daily walks past, without a second glance, the flag flying outside the public building. Millions of such barely glanced-at flags are on display each day. All these unmindful reminders are necessary for the continuation of the nation-state and for their members' sense of belonging.

Billig argues that when a group positions itself as a national group, its statements evoke an "ideological history of entitlements and rights" (219).

In his book *Being Danish*, the English sociologist Richard Jenkins examines national identity in Denmark, and he pinpoints five central themes this "danskhed"[2] is structured around: place, community, con-

---

2   Jenkins uses the Danish word "danskhed" in his work. The word can be translated to "Danishness" and encompasses significant traits in Danish national identity.

tinuity, reputation and institutions. Alongside Vikings and the myth about the Danish flag falling from heaven during a battle, he mentions Hans Christian Andersen as an example of the "feeling of historical continuity": "Even Hans Christian Andersen, relative newcomer as he is, contributes to the sense of time and timelessness" (Jenkins 220). Thus, Jenkins places Hans Christian Andersen as an element in Danish long-term identity, and he links the author with the statue of the Little Mermaid by emphasizing that the themes that structure Danish identity are all "symbolic and imagined":

> It is as symbols that these themes have their reality and power: symbols affect us as they do, and we hold to them as we do, at least in part because of the breadth and depth of the meanings condensed within them. Shared symbols work because they mean different things to different people. (223)

Jenkins thereafter identifies several "shared symbols", including the Little Mermaid, as material symbols that offer "a canopy of danskhed under which Danes, in all of their heterogeneity, with all of their paradoxes, can shelter from the sun as well as the rain, and under which they can proceed with everyday life without having to confront their differences too frequently". He further suggests that "it is precisely the imagined nature of danskhed that allows it to be a collective canopy" (224). From this viewpoint, the mermaid is a symbol open to different interpretations by different people.

In this paper, the Little Mermaid is contemplated as an "unmindful reminder" of national identity in Denmark, and when the Little Mermaid was moved to Shanghai, two predominant ways of speaking about the statue became evident in the media debate: in one discursive construction, the Little Mermaid was perceived as a tradable object, and in the other, it was perceived as a little girl. Both discourses contained various articulations of ownership regarding the statue, and, thus, the Little Mermaid was referred to as Danish cultural property.

Cultural property encompasses the physical artifacts in cultural heritage, and research on the concept is specifically concerned with the challenges that arise when movable cultural goods are being exchanged or withdrawn from exchange. A popular topic within the research on cultural property is the relation between the property object and the population it belongs to (Frow; Humphrey and Verdery). The anthropologists Humphrey and Verdery state that the entire concept of cultural property rests on this "homology between the group or 'people' and certain kinds of objects in which they see their identity as residing" (7). They have suggested that a certain property language is used in these situations and that it should be examined further how this language works by focusing on when a "phenomenon" is "called a matter of property, rather than something else" (11). The research on property language to date has been mainly concerned with minorities and their rights and fights to conserve and preserve their heritage from the ambient majority culture. There was no physical conflict when the Little Mermaid visited China, but the language used in Danish articulations about the exchange of it can still be categorized as a form of property language, as the Danish commentators were very eager to underline the fact that they experienced the statue as theirs. Based on the work of Humphrey and Verdery and Billig, respectively, this paper examines how articulations of appraisal and ownership in the two discursive constructions contained statements about central cultural values and cultural identity in Denmark.

The international body UNESCO has defined cultural heritage as a three-part concept, encompassing cultural property (physical artifacts), natural heritage (nature) and intangible culture (non-physical aspects of a culture) ("What is"; "Convention"). These three aspects were all parts of the Danish property language about the Little Mermaid. Some commentators defined the statue as *it*, a material artifact, that became the object of exchange between two countries. Other commentators brought the symbolic value of the Little Mermaid into focus by referring to it as a *she*, and in doing so, they simultaneously articulated traits that are specifically Danish. It will be argued that the content of this symbolic value illustrates how the meanings attached to the Little Mermaid reflected part of the intangible cultural heritage in Denmark. Natural heritage was also implicitly significant when the place dimension was broached among the commentators, as one of the most popular topics in this category was whether or not the Little Mermaid was significant because of its "natural environment" in Copenhagen Harbour. Thus, to examine how the Danes made sense of the Little Mermaid's participation in Expo 2010 is simultaneously to examine how the perceptions of tangible, intangible and natural cultural heritage interacted in this specific cultural context.

The following analysis of the appraisals of the Little Mermaid as they occurred in the Danish media debate will lead to a discussion about how the significance of the physical place of heritage was expressed in this media debate. The purpose of this paper is to attempt to answer the overall question: Can the cultural heritage come to the tourists or must the tourists always come to the cultural heritage?

Methodology

The analysis described in this paper was conducted as discourse analysis, especially inspired by Billig's contribution to the field. According to Billig, all psychological phenomena, including perceptions and emotions, are rooted in social and discursive activity ("Discursive" 212-213). The data reported in this paper are altogether a narrative about Danish perceptions of the Little Mermaid. In his analyses of national identity, Billig states that every utterance consists of "terms, which are culturally, historically and ideologically available" (217). The discourses about the Little Mermaid as a thing and a girl are analysed as discursive constructions, and when the commentators contributed to these discourses by appraising the Little Mermaid, they used property language.

The data were retrieved from a corpus of 884 units from the Danish media debate in 2009 and 2010. These units were collected using the advanced search function in the Danish media database, Infomedia, which covers 1693 Danish media sources. The data, however, are limited to articles from national newspapers, regional newspapers and releases from news agencies. These three media platforms are represented by 104 different sources in Infomedia. Furthermore, the search was limited to units that occurred within the time span 1 January 2009 till 31 December 2010. The string of words in the search on Infomedia was made as open as possible:

> Den lille Havfrue (exactly like this) (in the entire article) OG Shanghai (in the entire article) ELLER Expo (in the entire article)

This search generated 817 units. In order to make sure that no important articles or letters to the editor had been overlooked, the first search was supplemented with a string of words where "the Little Mermaid" was replaced with "the Mermaid", as this is a frequent designation of the statue in Denmark. This search brought the final total to 884 units. A preliminary analysis of random articles revealed the two dominant discourses about the Little Mermaid as "it" and "she", respectively. Based on the identification of these two thematic discourses, more data were added to the corpus until it was estimated that the material had reached the "saturation point", where new data did not contribute anything relevant and new about the content in and function of the two discourses (Bauer and Aarts 34).

In this paper, there are two instances of data which were not a part of the media debate in 2009 and 2010. One of them is the personal communication between the present writer and an employee from the municipality of Copenhagen about the insuring of the Little Mermaid in 2010. This official has, of course, given his consent for the publication of his statement as data. The other is a statement posted on a Chinese blog about the Little Mermaid in Shanghai. In China, there is a big difference between the public media debate and the actual attitude among the citizens, and this paper is specifically concerned with the latter. This highly relevant statement was only published in Chinese and was kindly sent to me by my colleague at the Fudan University in Shanghai, Ye Rulan, who also translated its content.

The Transformation from Property to Ownership

According to Humphrey and Verdery, property language is, among others, effectively used as an instrument for "the narrowing of 'property' to mean ownership" (11). This function was frequently present in the media debate about the Little Mermaid in Denmark, where the users of property language linked the statue to different "owners".

Technically, the municipality of Copenhagen owns the Little Mermaid. The statue was made because in 1909 the Danish brewer Carl Jacobsen had seen the ballerina Ellen Price as the Little Mermaid in a ballet based on Hans Christian Andersen's fairy tale. Jacobsen was enthralled by the ballerina and decided to have a statue of the mermaid made as a gift to the city of Copenhagen. When this *legal ownership* was articulated in the media in 2009 and 2010, the Little Mermaid was characterized as "the symbol of Copenhagen", "the icon of the city" and "possibly Copenhagen's most popular tourist attraction".[3] It was rarely mentioned that the statue legally belongs to the city, and

---

3   All short quotations in this paper stem from the Danish media debate in 2009 and 2010. The translations are mine.

the media debate reflects the fact that this actual ownership was not congruent with the perception of ownership among the commentators, who frequently placed the statue as "owned" by others.

Another articulated owner was the sculptor Edvard Eriksen, who made the Little Mermaid. He created the statue with Ellen Price as his source of inspiration but with his own wife as his model during the process. As Eriksen merely performed the task that Carl Jacobsen commissioned him to do, he did not legally own the Little Mermaid, but his responsibility for the existence of the statue was articulated in the media debate as an *artistic ownership* with expressions such as "Edvard Eriksen's pretty little sculpture" and "Edvard Eriksen's world-famous statue".[4] In the same category, some commentators linked the Little Mermaid to Hans Christian Andersen, who wrote the fairy tale about the mermaid long before the statue was made. These articulations referred to the Little Mermaid as "Hans Christian Andersen's fairytale figure" and not as a sculpture. In one of the contributions, Andersen's artistic ownership is phrased as "he who gave her life and breath – on paper – was Hans Christian Andersen" (Winge).

The Little Mermaid was not created to be a national treasure. When Eriksen finished the statue in 1913, it was placed on a rock on Langelinie in Copenhagen Harbour. It did not attract any noticeable attention until the 1930s, when the earliest links between Romanticism, Hans Christian Andersen, the Little Mermaid and Denmark surfaced in a tourism context. After the Second World War, the narrative about "the peaceful fairytale country" officially became the new foundation for Danish tourism and the statue of the Little Mermaid was the icon in the campaign. The new status as national icon in the global arena made the Little Mermaid a national treasure and a "must-see" for tourists who visited Denmark (Frausing).

The ownership that was presented most frequently in the media debate, however, was *national ownership.* A commentator stated that "Even though the Little Mermaid is owned by the municipality of Copenhagen on paper, she is actually owned by the people" (Hansen). This kind of ownership is not based on legal facts or tributes to the artists, but on a perception of the Little Mermaid as a national treasure

---

4   Actually, the copyright of any picture and reproduction of the Little Mermaid still belongs to the heirs of Eriksen. In that connection, it can be argued that a part of the statue as cultural property belongs to the Eriksen family. The permission to reproduce pictures of the Little Mermaid in this paper was also kindly given to the author by the Eriksen family.

that belongs to the nation. Thus, many commentators experienced the Little Mermaid as owned by "the Danes" and "Denmark". This ownership was based on emotions, and the contributions contained direct references to Denmark in terms such as "the national treasure", "the Danish monument", "Denmark's most famous mermaid", "Denmark's most famous attraction", "the Danish icon" and "the pride of Denmark". In some cases, the commentators phrased the same emotional relationship with indirect reference to Denmark and the Danes in expressions such as "our dearest possession", "our treasure" and "our biggest attraction".

When these perceptions of ownerships were used in the media debate, they structured two distinct narratives about the Little Mermaid. The most significant difference between the two narratives was the way they approached the question of appraisal in relation to the statue. Humphrey and Verdery accentuate that value is "central to any property relation of persons and things", because "no one wants to establish social relationships with respect to things of no value" (12). Where the articulations of the legal and to some extent also the artistic ownership referred to an exchange value of the mermaid, commentators who perceived the statue as owned by the people used descriptions of its symbolic and cultural value in their articulations.

In order to examine significant traits in the property language about the Little Mermaid, the following section will look further into how these appraisals made the Little Mermaid a matter of property in two different ways.

The Little Mermaid as an Object

Humphrey and Verdery have indicated that another function of property language is its effectiveness as an instrument in a process of commodification (11). In the discourse in which the Little Mermaid was referred to as "it", the commentators characterized the mermaid as "a statue", "a sculpture", and "a figure". In the Expo context, the Little Mermaid was thereby perceived as an object that was to be exchanged between two countries. Consequently, many of the commentators appraised the Little Mermaid's exchange value. The Head of The Danish Cultural Institute in China phrased his scepticism in this way: "The Mermaid is just a tourist attraction in Denmark. There is not much go in bringing an alien tourist attraction to the city. [...] A small and

The Little Mermaid was moved from its original spot on Langelinie in Copenhagen Harbour in March 2010. (Photo: Christian Alsing. Retrieved from copenhagenmediacenter.com)

almost 100-year-old bronze sculpture does not have many chances to create attention" (Olsen and Nielsen).

When the Little Mermaid visited Shanghai, it did attract attention, however, and maybe this was because the majority did not perceive the statue as just "a small and almost 100-year-old bronze sculpture". A member of the Technical and Environmental Committee in Copenhagen phrased his evaluation as follows: "I have always thought of the Little Mermaid as an overrated attraction, and the value the mermaid will infuse the World Exhibition with will by far surpass what we miss out on in Copenhagen" (Larsen). In this quote, the Little Mermaid is placed as an object of appraisal by the use of the word "overrated", and the commentator consequently considers its exchange value by his comparison of the statue's respective values in Copenhagen and in Shanghai. Another commentator first stated that "exchange of works of art is an everyday occurrence", but afterwards continued with this comment:

> In this context there is no difference between the Little Mermaid and a painting by Vilhelm Hammershøi. They are both parts of Danish culture. And of course they can both be lent out in relevant contexts where the aim is to exhibit Danish character, culture and tradition. (Hagmund)

By stating that there is "no difference" between the Little Mermaid and a painting of Hammershøi, the commentator merely addresses the mermaid as a material object, but afterwards he implicitly suggests a close relation between exchange value and the culturally specific symbolic value when he emphasizes that the Little Mermaid is not just a random cultural object but a representative of Danish culture and tradition. Within the field of research on cultural property, Maine has introduced a classic distinction between movable and immovable goods (204). As a consequence of modern market relations and value transformations, other researchers have subsequently pointed out that in some contexts the distinction must be enhanced with consideration of the alienability/inalienability of a given item (Rowlands; Weiner). The latter distinction allows for the individual experience of a cultural object as tradable or untradable. Within this frame of reference, the commentator in the above contribution perceives the Little Mermaid as a (temporarily) alienable thing that can represent "Danish character, culture and tradition" when it is exchanged.

This commentator and the committee member were both positive about the idea of moving the Little Mermaid to Shanghai, and in their arguments, they both referred to Denmark as a little country that must market itself in the best possible way in the global arena. Some scholars have placed inalienability as an introvert concept that threatens this free exchange between countries (Posey 42), and when other commentators were emotional in their viewpoints, their contributions often contained a negative opinion about the move. A commentator expressed this emotional dimension as follows: "Have you ever heard anything like it? Just like that, you move a national symbol and one of the most Danish things we have" (Adriansen). In this contribution, emotionality and the experience of national ownership are articulated simultaneously, but the Little Mermaid is still referred to as a thing. This was not the most frequent way of designating the Little Mermaid when the statue was articulated as owned by the nation, as it will be illustrated in the exposition of the alternative discourse below.

Rowlands is one of the scholars who states that inalienability traditionally has been seen as a "'backward' form of collective ownership" (207), but he is more concerned with the variability of distinctions between alienability and inalienability over time and how these two categories can both be implicit in the appraisal of cultural property. His further considerations are expressed as follows:

> [...] it scarcely matters whether 'control of one's own culture' is really about keeping cultural knowledge to oneself alone or is a means of claiming a form of property that can generate a unique form of exchange value. It is the inalienable and collective quality of cultural property that makes this a different form of value and orders social relations as a collective right to lay claim to its possession and to profit from this. (208)

In this quote, Rowlands mentions "a unique form of value" that stems from the experience of inalienability, but still embraces the culture's right to profit from it collectively.

However, when it was decided to move the Little Mermaid to Shanghai, the administration in the municipality of Copenhagen had to think of the statue as an object and put a price on it in order to get it properly insured. The price of the Little Mermaid was set at 10 million Danish kroner. But in emails sent to the present writer the employee who was responsible for fixing the mermaid's exchange value reveals that this reflected a complex valuation process. In one of the emails, the employee emphasized that "the valuation is naturally fictive. It is possible to make a new copy for a smaller amount of money because the original model still exists.[5] Thus, this valuation is based on other parameters, such as affective value, tourist attraction and cultural heritage". Moreover, he added that in this process of valuation, "you always choose a high and round number in order to indicate that special value that goes beyond the material value" (Munk).

Many property language users who referred to the Little Mermaid as an object, a tradable statue, did not leave much room for this "affective value" that the statue has for many Danes. Instead, they contributed to a narrative that was structured around the exchange, and the purpose of this exchange was to create profit for Denmark on a global level. In this discursive construction, the Little Mermaid was commoditized as a medium for obtaining this purpose.

The Little Mermaid as a Subject

The emotional dimension in the appraisal of the Little Mermaid was the crucial aspect of the other discourse, where the contributors frequently articulated the mermaid's symbolic value and perceived the statue as owned by the nation. In this narrative, the statue was designated as "she": a girl, woman or lady, who thereby was the subject in the contributions. A commentator integrated the transformation from object to subject as follows:

> The most photographed attraction in the country has never been a great work of art. She is and always will be a mannequin with a fish's tail. But to some extent, even dolls own a soul. Dolls are alive. As of today she will even see Shanghai. She will become one of the main attractions at the Expo. [...] But she will return home in December. (Schauser)

In this quote, the Little Mermaid is first of all equipped with a "soul" and a "home", and she is also given the ability to "see Shanghai". Where the narrative about the statue as an object was a narrative about business and experience economy, this narrative was closer to

---

5   The plaster cast of the Little Mermaid has on several occasions been used to restore the statue after vandalism.

a fairy tale. The architect who conceived the idea of moving the Little Mermaid described his perception of the statue as follows:

> There is no reason to cocoon our national treasures. But there is no reason to disown them either. It is, on the contrary, exciting to have a society where the symbols are not dead things but can be a little, living mermaid who can travel all the way to China if she feels like it. (Halgreen)

Apart from being an effective instrument in commodification contexts and in transforming property into ownership, Humphrey and Verdery associate the use of property language with processes of individualization (11). This function was evident in the narrative where the Little Mermaid was the subject, as many of the contributions contained arguments originating from specific Danish values and Danish national identity.

Even though the Little Mermaid was created as a tribute to a ballerina, many Danes linked her directly to Hans Christian Andersen who originally wrote the fairy tale about her. The discourse about the Little Mermaid as an object rarely referred to Hans Christian Andersen and only by means of the artistic ownership, but the link between the author and the figure was more emphatic when the statue was articulated as a female subject. When these commentators described the mermaid and the exchange of her, they were often inspired by the fairy tale. Just before the Little Mermaid was moved to Shanghai, a journalist used the fairy tale as follows in an article: "In the fairy tale by Hans Christian Andersen she is transformed into foam, but in reality the Little Mermaid will now be transformed into a Chinese" (Grønbech). Other commentators described the statue as "a delicate little woman", "shy", "thoughtful" and "wistful". When an illustration of the Little Mermaid was on the front page of the Shanghai Daily, a Danish journalist wrote as follows about the picture:

> The Mermaid has always radiated melancholy and mild grief, so it is not possible to see if she is sitting there with homesickness, missing the homely atmosphere. But according to the picture in the newspaper she is surrounded by Asians just like she used to be on Langelinie, so, in spite of all, something is like it used to be for the flighty lady. (Kruhøffer)

Descriptions inspired by the fairy tale were often emotional at the same time, and this emotionality was in many cases linked directly to articulations of national ownership. Thus, by means of Hans Christian Andersen's work and language, the Little Mermaid was transformed into a little girl who was going to travel for the first time in her life. This journey was described in picturesque phrases in the media debate, beginning before the departure with comments such as the following:

> I wonder if the Little Mermaid on Langelinie is ready to leave her usual spot and go away to represent Denmark in Asia for the next six months. She has confided in me that she is ready for the task and she added with a smile: 'A real mermaid does not turn its tail!' (Bramsen)

In this quote, the Little Mermaid is presented as a girl with the ability to speak and to "confide" in other human beings. With these traits added to the mermaid, the physical moving of her can appear to be violent: "There she hung – hovering in the air with hoists and straps and everything. But there was something magical about it anyway" (Vesterberg).

When the statue was revealed in Shanghai, even traits with sexual undertones were attached to it, when several Danish newspapers used the headline "The Little Mermaid Undressed for China" and further described her as "scantily dressed". Others were more genuine in their reports from Shanghai: "The Little Mermaid sits there in the middle of everything as we know her. A little shy on three big rocks and surrounded by seawater from Copenhagen" (Rytgaard). Even though the latter journalist avoids being too intimate, the use of the phrase "as we know her" is still very emotional and even caring. When these emotions were combined with emotions related to the nation, the descriptions could be even more voluminous. A Dane who visited the pavilion in Shanghai wrote a letter to the editor in which he described his observations of a Chinese family who visited the pavilion at the same time as him: "After he, his wife and daughter have spent more than an hour in queue, the family walks directly towards her, the pride of Denmark, the symbol of the fairy tale in our lovely country; The Little Mermaid, who is sitting on her rock in everlasting melancholia [...]" (Nielsen).

These descriptions are clear examples of how another kind of appraisal was dominant when the Little Mermaid was perceived as a "doll with a soul". The commentators did not refer to any kind of exchange value or profit from moving a cultural object – it was merely the symbolic value attached to the Little Mermaid that was articulated. Even when economic themes were addressed, the mermaid was still referred to as a person and not as a thing with a price: "The Little Mermaid will be equipped with a huge budget when she becomes one of the prominent Danish guests at the World Exhibition in Shanghai" (Roest-Madsen) was one of the expressions where economy and mermaid were effectively separated.

The symbolic value was very clearly articulated when the media fairy tale ended and, finally, the Little Mermaid "returned home" safely from her journey to the other side of the world. A commentator stated that he had "missed her so much" and that "she should never have been sent away", because "it is like selling a part of your soul" (Frandsen, "Hvor har vi savnet dig"). And a politician from the City Council in Copenhagen used the same terminology about the homecoming: "It is wonderful that she has come home. She has been missed so much. It has been like sending your child away. [...] She fascinates me, and she is like a fairy tale" (Frandsen, "Hvor har vi savnet dig").

The Little Mermaid is undoubtedly endowed with a great deal of symbolic value in these articulations, and it is evident that the perception of a national ownership accelerated the use of a highly emotional property language about the statue. Even when the commentators tried to switch these feelings off, they still connected the statue to their national identity, as is the case in this formulation:

> You don't need to be at the World Exhibition for long, before you understand that your Danish identity resides on a pretty hard rock in a fairly chic pavilion these days: To the Chinese people, Denmark is identical with the Little Mermaid, and then it doesn't matter whether you feel related to Hans Christian Andersen's little [fish scale] lady or not. (Goul; my correction)

Since the articulations of the symbolic value attached to the statue in Danish media reflected a discursive construction of the Little Mermaid as a female (Danish) subject, it can be argued that the function of this discourse was that it constituted a mild "process of individualization" (Humphrey and Verdery 11), because the commentators were very eager to accentuate what Billig terms their "right" to the mermaid, and as they did so, they simultaneously highlighted Denmark as a unique place with a unique interpretation of the Little Mermaid. And in many cases, this interpretation contained viewpoints of the statue as immovable and inalienable. Thereby, this discourse can be seen as an example of how the Little Mermaid functions as an "unmindful reminder" of national identity in Denmark.

The Significance of Place

The two discursive constructions function as expressions of the local level in the global-local fusion that occurred when the Little Mermaid was moved to Shanghai. This section will look further into how the physical place of heritage was implemented in the Danish property language, when the commentators attached and detached the statue to and from the physical place of heritage in their articulations.

When the Little Mermaid was articulated as an object, the commentators and journalists concentrated on the process of moving the statue. One journalist emphasized the importance of moving the entire location with the statue to China:

> The location of the Little Mermaid and the rocks it rests on is measured in advance with punctual laser equipment. It ensures that the siting in China will be as it is in Denmark. At the same time it means that the old lady will get the exact same view as she is used to when she returns to her spot on Langelinie after six months in the East. (Jensen)

The move from place to place is described but not problematized in this contribution. There is an interesting shift in the quote, though: When the journalist writes about moving the Little Mermaid to China, the statue is described as an object surrounded by words such as "measure" and "punctual laser equipment". But when he describes the statue's homecoming after the exposition, it becomes an "old lady" to whom it matters whether the view is "the exact same" as "she is used to".

As mentioned earlier, UNESCO's three-part definition of cultural heritage also includes a natural dimension. When some of the commentators emphasized the immovable elements in the Little Mermaid, they related the statue to the environment in which it is placed in Denmark, and when they did so, their contributions were often more emotional. One commentator stated that the mermaid "is alive because of its placement" (Holm), and another expressed it as follows: "The Little Mermaid's forte is exactly the surroundings she naturally finds herself in. If you move her to Disneyland, she is nothing" (Hansen). This commentator physically placed the symbolic value of the mermaid on the rocks in Copenhagen Harbor. A strategic director expressed the same concern in his contribution to the debate:

> As a PR instrument, the Little Mermaid runs the risk of drowning. As a symbol she will lose her cultural power and significance in alien surroundings. After all, the status of the bashful little girl is attached to her rock and the view over Øresund from Langelinie. Away from her familiar surroundings she will hardly attract the same attention as that we ascribe to her. (Gjerløff)

As these contributions illustrate, the physical place of heritage was frequently mentioned in the media debate in accentuations of the Little Mermaid's symbolic value, and by means of the statue's emplacement in Danish culture and in Denmark, it was articulated as immovable and inalienable. Even so, on 25 March 2010, the tangible cultural property was removed from Copenhagen Harbour and transported to the exposition in Shanghai where it was admired by more than five million Chinese people. Its exchange value was randomly fixed at 10 million Danish kroner. But as the Little Mermaid went global with all its exchange value, its Danish "cultural power", as it was termed in the media debate, remained in its natural element on the rocks in Copenhagen Harbour. Thus, the Little Mermaid arrived in Shanghai without its habitual symbolic value and was therefore open to new appraisals and interpretations from the Chinese heritage tourists visiting the Expo 2010.

The Chinese fascination with the Little Mermaid is based on a specific Chinese symbolic valuation of the statue, as the Little Mermaid is solely perceived as a reflection of Hans Christian Andersen. The Chinese people term Andersen as "An Tusheng", and this can be translated as "born into a poor family" (Ye Rulan, "HCA in China"). In an argument about what the Chinese people can learn from Hans Christian Andersen's fairy tales, the Chinese scholar Guo Dehua has illustrated how Hans Christian Andersen's fairy tales are read as a wise man's advice on how to cope with life, death, love and sorrow. She argues that "Hans Christian Andersen is popular here in China because he has seen through society and its roles. His intelligence transcends cultural boundaries, for Andersen deals with human themes" (Guo Dehua).

The statue was placed in the middle of a basin in the Danish pavilion in Shanghai, where it was an attraction for six months. (Photo: Torben Grøngaard Jeppesen)

Another Chinese citizen expressed a similar experience of the mermaid on her blog after visiting the Danish pavilion at the Expo:

> Many think the real beauty of the Little Mermaid doesn't lie in the visual effect. She's of great value because of Andersen who created her story. The culture is being passed just like vintage wine, the older the mellower. And the journey of the Little Mermaid to China (...) stimulates those who are familiar with Andersen to re-read his writings, and attracts those who haven't read the story of the Little Mermaid to pick up the book. What impressed a lot of the audience is that the seemingly lifeless statue sparkles with living sadness and beauty all over her. (Ye Rulan, private email)

When the Te Maori exhibition opened in New York, the tangible Maori culture was defined as fine art by the Metropolitan Museum of Art. And in a similar way, the Little Mermaid was experienced in Chinese as a material reflection of Andersen's fairy tales when it was moved to Shanghai. In both cases, the fact that the cultural heritage was displaced from its natural habitat gave room for these new interpretations.

Conclusions and Recommendations

This paper has examined the loan of the Little Mermaid as an act of glocal heritage tourism, because a tangible part of Danish cultural heritage was moved to a present field of global interest when the statue became a part of the Danish pavilion at the exposition in Shanghai 2010. The purpose of this paper was to analyse language use concerning the Little Mermaid in the Danish media debate in 2009 and 2010. The notion that a particular property language is used when individuals articulate meaning about their cultural heritage as property was applied as a framework for the analysis.

This paper suggests that at least three kinds of ownership were articulated in the Danish media debate about the Little Mermaid: a legal, an artistic, and a national ownership. The analysis was concerned with how these three ownership types were articulated in two discursive constructions within the Danish property language: a discourse in which the Little Mermaid was perceived as an object of exchange and a discourse in which the Little Mermaid was represented as a female person. These two discourses have in common the characteristic that appraisal is a central part of the language use. The commentators and journalists who experienced the statue as an object appraised its exchange value, while the media users who contributed to the discourse about the Little Mermaid as a subject referred to its symbolic value. The analysis made evident that central values in Danish culture and identity were at stake in both categories of appraisals, but while this experience of national ownership was only one element among others in the first discourse, it was a fundamental part of the latter. This paper suggests that the culturally specific symbolic value of the Little Mermaid was fixed: the fact that the contents of the symbolic appraisals were so closely linked to the way that the Danes experience their common national identity positioned the Little Mermaid as a reflection of intangible cultural heritage in Denmark. This was also indicated in the part of the analysis where the commentators connected the Little Mermaid to its "natural environment" in Copenhagen Harbour. Thus, as the Little Mermaid was detached from its habitual symbolic value at the Expo 2010 in Shanghai, the Chinese audience was able to appraise the statue's value in its own culturally specific way.

As this paper has only been concerned with two discourses in the Danish property language, there may be other elements of property language about global-local fusions within heritage tourism left untouched. Topics of interest in future analyses of this could be, for example, the content and function of discursive constructions about the importance (or unimportance) of heritage authenticity or the meaning-making of heritage out of place that occurs when visitors experience the heritage in question.

Acknowledgements

This paper was first presented in outline at the workshop "The National and Cultural Significance of Hans Christian Andersen" held at the Fudan University in Shanghai, China, in November 2011. I thank the participants from Fudan and from the University of Southern Denmark for their comments, especially my colleague, lecturer and PhD Ye Rulan, who helped me with Chinese translation and important links. Another helper is Affiliate Research Professor Thomas Pettitt, University of Southern Denmark, who proofread my paper. I have also benefited from valuable insights and thoughts from my supervisor, Professor Nils Gunder Hansen, University of Southern Denmark, and from Professor Thomas Hylland Eriksen, University of Oslo. Last, but definitely not least, I thank the extremely qualified and engaged anonymous reviewers of Journal of Heritage Tourism, where this paper was originally published.

Chinese Interpretations of Andersen's Fairy Tales

Li Hongye
Guest Professor at the Hans Christian Andersen Center, University of Southern Denmark, from the Department of Chinese Language and Literature, Hunan University of Humanities, Science and Technology

"Andersen"! How much it conjures up in Chinese! It sounds intimate and familiar, it evokes an inexpressibly tender feeling and aspiration, like the warm sunshine on a spring afternoon caressing new twigs, or like a mother's hand touching her baby's face, or else, a miracle that has befallen, bringing us to primordial existence and bliss, to Mother Nature's bosom. Pronouncing the name resembles the whispering of one's hidden soul, at once *déjà vu* yet brand new! Andersen is a noun, it stands both for a fairytale poet from Denmark at the other end of the world, and for his fairy tales, and in a larger perspective for all the fairy tales in the world. Andersen is also an adjective, descriptive of all the fantastic experiences, beautiful scenes, and sweet feelings. Yes, it is intimate to us, like any handy cultural product with which we are familiar.

Let us reidentify the cultural implications of the word Andersen in a Chinese context.[1] Hans Christian Andersen (1805-1875) is the first Danish writer that won international acclaim in the 19th century. His extraordinary imagination first manifested itself in drama and novels, but was soon expressed in fairy tales. Once he turned to the composition of fairy tales, a miracle was bound to take place and ensure him a colossal world reputation. He made a breakthrough from the popular norm of the tales of the Brothers Grimm by introducing personal imagination and realistic elements into the genre, thus opening up new vistas for the genre's modern form.

---

[1] This paper is from an abstract of my book *Chinese Interpretations of Andersen's Fairy Tales* (Beijing: China Peace Publishing House, 2005). The manuscript of the book was completed in April 2004, the abstract in English in September 2004.

Andersen's tales are based on the author's rich experience in life, and are expressive of a humanitarian, positive and optimistic attitude towards life. The author sings of Nature and childhood innocence; rejoices in love and beauty; delights in the soul's repose; and sighs over banality and spiritual degeneration. His multifaceted aesthetics comprises sweet fantasies, light merriment, mild humour, acrid irony, and profound sorrow, as well as religious piety and human gratitude for divine grace.

Andersen is so talented that he is capable of communicating to children the universe's multifarious phenomena in the most direct and succinct manner, and of expressing complicated human experiences and worldly affairs in innocent children's language. His natural child-like tone, his agility in moving freely between animal and botanical lives and ordinary phenomena, infinite marvels, and a desire for perfection – all these make Andersen a pioneer of children's literature. However, the readership of Andersen's tales is not restricted to children. The author's most moving characteristic lies in his marvellous ability to express the first encounter with the world, in his sincere sympathy and sharp observation of things, his awareness of life's limitations, and his untiring search for eternity. All these elements combine together to endow his tales with an unmistakably poetic quality. Thus from a simple, lucid and unsophisticated text, children are able to see the marvels of things as well as the joy and love contained therein, whilst adults can recognize their vanished childhood and perceive the poetry and mystery of things. For almost two hundred years, Andersen has won the love of both children and adults all over the world; and his tales, with their lasting appeal, have become the cultural and spiritual heritage of humankind as a whole.

The circulation and reading of Andersen's fairy tales in China is a most significant phenomenon in the history of reading. Andersen is also one of the best known and beloved foreign writers in China. His fairy tales are "pets" of Chinese kindergarten kids, and are required reading for primary and secondary school pupils, and, according to recent research, Andersen's fairy tales have been deemed to be one of "the fifty books that have moved the readers in the People's Republic of China." (*Chuban guangjiao*).

As early as 1913, Zhou Zuoren, chief campaigner of the New Cultural Movement, introduced Andersen into China. During the May Fourth Modernist Era, Chinese literati made every effort to promulgate and popularize his fairy tales, so introducing and translating Andersen's tales were regarded as a major cultural project in the 1920s. In 1925, the renowned magazine *Xiaoshuo yuebao* (The Short Story Magazine) published unprecedentedly two special issues featuring Andersen.

The 1950s saw the publication of the complete works of Andersen in Chinese translation. All these efforts made his tales widely read and the Danish author well known to almost every family in the country. The rich quality of children's literature inherent in Andersen's tales has inspired Chinese writers and given birth to Chinese children's literature. His works have become the norm for writers to follow, adhere to, and, as the critic Wang Quangen observes, "Learning from Andersen has become an essential and integral part of self-cultivation for Chinese writers of fairy tales." (938).

The reception of Andersen's fairy tales in China and their far-reaching influence on Chinese writers' creation, especially of children's literature, constitute a unique cross-cultural phenomenon on the 20th century Chinese literary scene. Unfortunately, this remarkable phenomenon has not received due attention from the academic community. The close rapport between Andersen and the Chinese as well as its function in Chinese cultural construction has not been systematically studied, nor can existing studies of the tales themselves match the great reputation of their author. In China, in the huge database of literary studies, the entry under Andersen is deplorably meagre, and in the fully stocked libraries, one cannot find even a single tome on Andersen that lives up to the elite standard of contemporary scholarship.

Therefore, one can safely say that Andersen studies in China remain unchartered terrain. The reason is by no means hard to find: Traditional norms of literary studies have centered around "adult" writing, and Andersen has been thus pushed to the periphery of what is labelled children's literature; on the other hand, a research culture for children's literature, including the fairy tale and fantasy literature, has not yet been fully established.[2] Under these circumstances, my book *Chinese Interpretations of Andersen's Fairy Tales* tries to play a challenging role in bridging the aforementioned research gap. By

---

2 Another important reason is language barriers which make it difficult for a Chinese researcher to get a first-hand account. Apart from a few translators, such as Ye Junjian, Lin Hua, Shi Qin'e, few scholars understand Danish. One who can neither directly read Andersen's works in the original, nor follow the the most recent Danish research on Andersen, has to rely on a few texts translated from Danish or English.

providing a comprehensive survey of the reception of Andersen, the man and his work in China over the past hundred years, the book aims at reconstructing the factual and spiritual rapports between China and the Danish writer. In terms of the quantity of information, the book roughly corresponds to the scale of an Andersen encyclopedia in China. With regard to methodology, the book appropriates the method of influence and reception studies of comparative literature and employs models of cross-cultural studies. Through a thorough investigation of Andersen's fortune in China, the book has carved a Chinese image out of the alien texts by Andersen. It is my belief that as soon as the long and winding road of cross-cultural transmission has been mapped out, as soon as the dialogic interaction between two cultures has been reenacted, both the message-emitting "Other" and the receiving "Self" will be endowed with novel significance relevant to our times.

The reception of Andersen in China is not unlike that in other countries. Because of his extensive influence in the realm of children's reading, the author's other achievements[3] are often ignored. In China, our recognition of children's mentality was initiated by Andersen's tales. Children's reading experience starts with Andersen. His tales first belong to children, and to children's literature. No other literary corpus is more important in the genesis of children's literature in China, in children's development, and in serving as a more powerful frame of reference. The various themes and devices have been adopted and reincarnated in Chinese children's literature at different historical moments. Such themes and devices include the lyrical keynote, the characters' craving for love and beauty, the narrator's sympathy towards the underprivileged, the use of non-human characters, fantasies, personification, all encoded in a gentle tone and the language of a child. All these survive in their Chinese variations.

The borrowed textuality of Andersen's tales, despite its circulation of about a century in China, has not been properly and fully recognized. Among the two hundred tales that have been rendered into Chinese, only a few have really become and innate part of our knowledge. There is a set of rather stereotyped impressions about the Chinese reception. Here I will give a few examples. The Romantic characteristics and imaginative quality of Andersen have been identified as consonant

---

3   Such as novels, plays, poems, travel books, papercuts, collages, drawings, and so on.

with the ideal qualities that the architects of the New Literature in the early 20th-century China were seeking. On the other hand, these characteristics are thought to be incompatible with the traditional values of literature at the service of politics, of patriarchy and collectivism, etc. All these complications resulting from cultural clashes have led to different images of Andersen. Andersen has been labelled as a "perpetual boy", "old dotard writing in the garden", "master of Realism", "maestro of canonical children's literature", "speaker of mind and soul", "childish adult", and so on and so forth.

There is no denying that an imported writer, like local writers, is always subject to infinite representations, depending on the receivers' respective horizons of expectation, which are historically conditioned. Under these circumstances, Andersen has been substantially enriched in China, but at the same time, the intrinsic beauty of Andersen as a writer of fairy tales is lost. Researchers like myself are seeking to reduce this paucity of research. We hope that serious and full-scale scholarly studies focusing on the aesthetic value of Andersen as a classic canon of children's literature, and of literature in general, will thrive and bloom in 21st-century China.

Andersen has become one of the most well-known foreign authors in China because of his profound humanitarianism, and his tales transcend linguistic borders. The incarnation of love, perseverance and sacrifice of the Little Mermaid has made thousands of Chinese readers shed tears. She is not only a symbol of Denmark, but also a statue for worship in the Chinese spiritual shrine. "The Little Match Girl" has evoked an infinite sense of pity among its Chinese readers, and has therefore entered the list of required school reading, not to mention the fact that it has inspired dozens of imitators. Perhaps no tale is more popular than "The Emperor's New Clothes" because of its political and social satire; it is so popular that it has even become a *cliché populaire* in Chinese. "The Ugly Duckling" is another tale that has become a Chinese idiomatic expression. Many a Chinese sees in the duck his or her own image, and having learnt about the tale's autobiographical background, tends to identify with its author. This collective identification of Andersen as a family member in China testifies to the prolonged suffering of the Chinese people since the nineteenth century and their craving for a brighter future.

Reading Andersen is unarguably the most memorable experience. The fact that the author is not yet extensively studied in the academic community does not annul his phenomenal popularity among his readership. The tender love and fabulous marvels repose quietly in the deep recesses of our souls. Reading Andersen amounts to some kind of physical and mental settling down, cleansing and baptism, precisely because it evokes the best and most beautiful part of human feelings. It is such feelings that arm us against the basic human instinct towards selfishness and human vulnerability to utilitarianism. This is what I term "fairytale spiritualism". Like literature, fairytale spiritualism is capable of elevating us and transporting us to a better and more meaningful way of living. This is one of the cultural implications of Andersen's reception in China.

A Discussion on Political Appropriation of Andersen's Fairy Tales in China

Zhu Jianxin
Associate Professor, Research Fellow of the Nordic
Literature Research Institute, Fudan University

Most readers outside Denmark read Hans Christian Andersen's fairy tales through translated texts. As translation is not only an interlingual transformation but also an intercultural communication, Andersen's originals have undergone a process of transmutation when they enter a new language and a new culture. As a key part of culture, ideology can exert an influence on translation in a comprehensive way. To a large extent, it determines the choice of the translated text and the translation strategy. The translated text, on the other hand, can inform the dominant ideology of a society at the time when it is translated. In *Translation, Rewriting and Manipulation of Literary Fame*, Andre Lefevere argues that "Translation is, of course, a rewriting of an original text. All rewritings, whatever their intention, reflect a certain ideology and poetics and as such manipulate literature to function in a given society in a given way" (preface). The manipulation of ideology can also be illustrated in highly distinctive or even freewheeling interpretations of the translated text at a different historical moment, and in a different social situation and cultural climate.

The political appropriation of foreign literature existed in China long before Andersen's works were translated into Chinese. For example, the translation of foreign literary works in the late Qing Dynasty aimed at bringing in advanced Western thoughts for political reforms. Yan Xiaoiang claims that Yan Fu's translation of social science works tries to "awaken a democratic and revolutionary consciousness of intellectuals through translation" (64) in China during the late Qing and early Republican periods. The translation and interpretation of Andersen's fairy tales in China were appropriated politically in a similar fashion.

Taking the Chinese translation of "The Little Match Girl" (1845) and "The Emperor's New Clothes" (1837) as primary examples, the paper attempts to investigate how the translation and reception of Andersen's tales have been manipulated to serve political ends in different political environments in China.

"The Emperor's New Clothes" is the first Andersen tale that was translated into Chinese. It appeared in the 7th issue of the literary magazine *Chinese Novel* in 1914 but under a new title, "A Big Fan of Foreign Stuff" (*Yangmixiaolou*). The translator Liu Bannong (1891-1934) not only changed the title but the story as well. In this adapted version of Andersen's original, the protagonist is no longer an emperor but a returned student from abroad. He is so infatuated with foreign goods that everything including his food, clothes and other life necessities such as a chamber pot is imported. He even wishes that one day he himself could be transformed into a Westerner by some magic power. One day he receives two foreigners. They claim to be great weavers from the West who have just invented a kind of magic fabric. The magic power possessed by the fabric is able to help the student to tell a good person from a bad person. They tell him that the fabric will become more beautiful seen by a good person; while seen by a bad person, the fabric will immediately turn invisible. As they learn that he has a particular fondness of foreign stuff and great admiration for new inventions, they decide to travel to China to present their newly invented fabric to him. Needless to say, the two visitors are crooks and they easily hoax the returned student into buying their fabric. Finally, the returned student becomes an object of ridicule when he strolls around naked, showing off his latest acquisition. In order to help the Chinese readers to better understand his rewriting of the Anderson's world-famous story, Liu explained his intention in the preface of his translation:

> Now, according to Chinese convention, I only try to capitalize on the meaning of the original of Andersen and Japanese play (i.e. *The New Clothes* adapted from Andersen's fable "The Emperor's New Clothes" to Japanese) to criticize those who are infatuated with foreign things. My intention is to reflect the truth, not to weed through the original and bring forth the new. (Guo Yanli 481)

Then, what truth does Liu want to reflect? Why does the protagonist change from an emperor into a returned student? Due to the humiliating defeat in the Opium War and ensuing unequal treaties in the 1840s, the Chinese rulers and officials were forced to recognize the need to strengthen the country. In order to defend China from further acts of foreign aggression, the officials and scholars launched a reform programme, the so-called "Self-strengthening Movement" (1861-1895), to modernize the nation by learning from the West. During the four-decade-long modernization process, Western science and languages were studied, modern schools were opened, and factories were established according to Western models. At the same time, students were sent abroad by the government and on individual or community initiatives in the hope that national regeneration could be achieved through the application of Western practical methods. However, all the efforts failed to arrest the decline of the Qing Dynasty or stop foreign powers from carving up the empire continuously. Frustrated by the increasing foreign influences, the angry peasants from northern areas launched the Boxer Uprising in 1898 aimed at driving the foreigners, especially foreign missionaries, out of the country. When the rebellion was finally quelled by an international force in 1900, suspicion, hatred and fear of foreigners began to intensify in the whole country. After the downfall of the Qing Dynasty and the founding of the Republic of China in 1911, the anti-foreign element still remained strong. Sun Yat-sen, founder of the Republic, called for the nation to restore the national spirit and recreate historical grandeur.

Published in 1914 when the cultural revival and restoration was a crucial issue in national political life, "A Big Fan of Foreign Stuff" manifested the political atmosphere on the eve of a great cultural movement, featuring the return of the conservatives who had opposed the Western intrusion since the middle of the 19th century. Unlike traditional conservatives, those Republican conservatives did not seek to protect a feudal dynasty and its Confucian commitment but sought to protect what they believed to be the "national heritage", the cultural legacy as constituted in China's long history. However, those students who were sent to study abroad during the Self-strengthening Movement returned home advocating social and political reform to westernize China and Chinese culture. To remove the menace of a ruthless and indiscriminate undermining of the cultural tradition of China and restore in the Chinese mind a sense of historical continuity, the conservatives began to use literature as a tool to reinforce the importance of tradition and affect the political, moral and educational attitudes in a period of unprecedented national emergency. Replacing the emperor with a returned student, Liu's rewriting of "The Emperor's New Clothes" not only addressed the political interests of Republican conservatives who were antagonistic to Western technology and democratic institutions but also ridiculed the attempt of the returned students to sever the country from its historical past. What is more, the image of emperor was no longer historically relevant in a time when the newly-founded Republic just ended a three-thousand-year feudal rule in China. It is also important to add that the fact that the story was translated into classical Chinese also reflected the conservatives' political commitment to the preservation of the Chinese literary tradition because they believed that classical Chinese was the last thread to maintain historical continuity.

Another political appropriation of "The Emperor's New Clothes" took place in the 1930s when Ye Shengtao (1894-1988), a famous writer of fairy tales in China, created a story of the same title based on Andersen's story. Ye's "The Emperor's New Clothes" (*Huangdi de Xinyi*) is included in his second collection of fairy tales, *The Stone Statue of an Ancient Hero* (*Gudai Yingxiong de Shixiang*, 1931). Ye begins his story from where Andersen's story ends: "And so he carried himself still more proudly, and the chamberlains held on more tightly than ever, and carried the train which did not exist at all" (92). Then Ye continues the story in his version: "What happened afterwards? Andersen did not say. Really there were many, many things." (Farquhar 109). After the child speaks out the truth, people find their emperor nothing but an ordinary man who looks particularly skinny, black and hairy. They start to laugh. Feeling humiliated, the angry emperor orders the immediate execution of anyone daring to criticize his clothes. As his tyranny grows, he even passes a law that forbids the people to talk or laugh in his presence. As a result, one thousand people including his favorite concubine and most loyal minister are killed because of their failure to obey his rules. One day, when he orders his soldiers to break into a house where a baby is crying and a woman singing, people rebel. They rush out of their homes, surround their emperor and torture him. Seeing the emperor sitting on the ground looking just like a monkey, the soldiers burst out laughing. Soon everyone is laughing and the emperor falls into a dead-like faint!

Despite the same title, the two stories differ significantly from each other. Ye's story is no longer a celebration of a child's innocence and criticism of adult's vanity. The humorous touch in Andersen's tale is also lost in Ye's version. Yet, Ye adds to Andersen's original a political dimension that goes well beyond the popular figure of the little boy. During the late 1920s, China was plagued with political disunity throughout the country. The Nationalist Party led by Chiang Kai-shek launched extermination campaigns against the Communists, which threw the country into a civil war. At the same time, former warlords challenged Chiang for the national leadership. Faced with the growing threat from Japan, many Chinese, especially students and intellectuals, called for the establishment of internal unity because they believed the continued civil war in China could only encourage Japanese aggressors. But in order to strengthen his dictatorship, Chiang insisted on exterminating the Communists first. In Mary Ann Farquhar's reading of Ye's story, she argues that the story manifested Ye's "disillusion, shared by many writers, over the split between the Nationalists and the Communists in 1927" (106), and his increasing disapproval of Chiang's dictatorship. In his "The Emperor's New Clothes", Ye ridiculed the authorities, who were arrogant and insensitive to his people, and called for a more radical solution. Under the actual circumstances, what the country needed to end the internal turmoil was a revolution. As Farquhar points out, according to Ye Shengtao, the best way to create a better society is "through revolutionary action" (107). Furthermore, people must unite to fight against social injustice as well as impending foreign aggression and that is the real road which will lead to peace and happiness.

The first Chinese translation of "The Little Match Girl" was published in 1919 when the New Culture Movement (1915-1921), an iconoclastic and anti-traditional movement, reached its climax. The translator was Zhou Zuoren. He was also the first person who introduced Andersen to Chinese readers in 1913. As an active participant of the New Culture Movement and a key figure in the May Fourth Movement, Zhou shared the belief that China should reject traditional values and selectively adopted ideals of science and democracy to strengthen the nation and thus advocated literary reform. In a 1918 article entitled "Literature of Humanity", he called for a "humanist literature" in which "any custom or rule that goes against human instincts and nature should be rejected or rectified" ("Zhou Zuoren", *Wikipidia*). To achieve such a goal, the independent personality of women and children should be recognized and respected. Translated into vernacular Chinese, emphasizing the children's perspective and published in the famous journal *New Youth*, Zhou's translation of "The Little Match Girl" was not only a solid step towards his ideal literature, which was both democratic and individualistic, but also an effective way to accommodate political demands at a time of drastic socio-political changes.

In feudal China, children were regarded as adults in miniature or the possession of adults. Their duty was to obey the teachings of their ancestors and so-called childhood teaching was no more than learning Confucian doctrines. During the New Culture Movement which articulated the contempt for traditional Chinese culture, the intellectuals educated in the West attacked everything that represented Confucianism, including traditional texts and approaches to child-raising and insisted on scientific attitudes towards children which recognized children's special characteristics and their distinctive needs. Therefore, they regarded the child-oriented and child-centred fairy tales from Western countries as a ready-made recipe for confronting the bulwark of Confucian education. Among them, they found Andersen an ideal author for advocating their revolutionary ideas. They were most impressed with Andersen's efforts not to use words that children might have difficulty in understanding and his great ingenuity in paraphrasing complicated words and ideas and conveying abstract ideas through a tangible reality. Furthermore, attaching great importance to children and recognizing their independent personality also answered the call in the New Culture Movement for an orientation towards the future rather than the past and an end to the patriarchal family in favour of individual freedom. In this logic, the world of fantasy created by Andersen could be an effective way to inspire children's creativity and influence their spiritual growth. Among his tales, "The Little Match Girl" provided a perfect story that fitted in the scenario of the Movement. The tale focuses on depicting unrealistic thoughts and ideas that only exist in the personal paradise of a child, where death comes as a relief to the mortals who are worn out by suffering and leads them to a warm world of eternal love and peace on a cold and lonely night.

The political significance of the Zhou translation of "The Little Match Girl" also lies in the language he used to translate Andersen's classical tale and the journal in which the tale was published. The intellectual attack against traditional Chinese culture in New Culture Movement was also aimed at the long-established linguistic hierarchy. Inspired by the story of emerging vernaculars during the European Renaissance, the intellectuals persistently promoted the use of vernacular Chinese and abandoned classical Chinese, the written language prior to the Movement, in literary practices, proclaiming that "a dead language cannot produce a living literature" (Zhou Gang, "Language, Myth, Identity" 362). To support the call for the adoption of the vernacular as the national language, *New Youth*, the most influential journal and a leading forum in China to promote the New Culture Movement, published articles that challenged the conventional linguistic vehicle possessed by men of letters and championed vernacular literature as canonical. As a result, the vernacular became "a loaded image, both literally and politically, representing all the hope and passion for a promising future" (Zhou Gang, "Language, Myth, Identity" 53). As the first Andersen tale translated into vernacular Chinese, Zhou's "The Little Match Girl" was imbued with his political commitment and democratic spirit. Under his pen, the untamed imagination of a pitiable young girl selling matches on New Year's Eve is rendered with the same humanistic touch and poetic sensitivity as Andersen's original in fresh and natural vernacular Chinese.

After the founding of the People's Republic in 1949, political ideology continued to exert tremendous influence on the translation and reception of Andersen's works, especially from the early 1950s to mid-1970s, when the translation of foreign literature was subject to tight censorship scrutiny, which upheld ideological criteria as opposed to artistic criteria. The translation, publication, circulation and reception of foreign literature were required to be conducive to the Communist Party's political agenda. At the National Convention of Translators in Beijing in 1954, Mao Dun, Minister of Culture and one of the most celebrated writers in modern Chinese literature put it explicitly in his report that translation should become a part of political activities and that translation activities should be guided by the Communist party and done systematically with plans and organisations (Meng Zhaoyi and Li Zaidong 294). The Communist leader Mao Zedong even said: "Let the past serve the present, let foreign things serve China." But how can a foreign writer of fairy tales as Andersen serve the political ends of New China?

In the first place, as the son of a poor cobbler and a washerwoman, Andersen was introduced to common readers in China as a proletarian writer who shared the same misery and suffering with poor people and his tales were then naturally categorized as part of proletarian literature, an art form developed by the proletariat as one of its weapons in the class struggle. Under the influence of Marxist ideology and Soviet critics, Chinese scholars, writers and literary critics tended to assess the political tendency of his tales. One typical way of assessment was to analyse how the class constructs were demonstrated under his pen. In this light, Chinese critics divided the characters in Andersen's tales into two groups: the ruling class, who were evil, cruel and stupid, and people of lower social status, who were real, kind and wise. Populating his stories with these two categories of characters, Andersen attacked the ruling class and exposed their evilness and stupidity while praising the virtues of working-class people and demonstrating his strong sympathy with their tragic experiences in life. Chen Bochui, a famous Chinese writer of children's literature, commented in his essay entitled "What We Should Learn from Andersen":

> He always sided with the working class. He loved all kind-hearted people. He showed compassion towards the small potatoes in a class-ridden society. He possessed a strong sense of justice. He hated all the enemies of the labouring people, the rulers and their walking dogs so much that he would take great pains to expose their evils. (69)

Ye Junjian, one of the best-known translators of Andersen's tales in China, expressed his viewpoint in a similar tone in the preface to his translation of Andersen's works in 1958. He said, "Andersen displayed such a strong hatred for the cruelty of the ruling class that he would lose no chance to ridicule their stupidity. On the other hand, he sang high praises for the wisdom and noble-mindedness of the working class" (91). For this reason, it is not hard to understand why "The Little Match Girl", a story about a girl from a poor family who freezes to death on New Year's Eve, and "The Emperor's New Clothes", in which a foolish ruler is humiliated in the presence of his subjects, are included in the textbook to become the two best circulated Andersen stories among readers in New China. In the eyes of the Communist leaders, no other Andersen tales can better illustrate the dark side of capitalist countries than these two.

During the interlingual and cross-cultural travel of Hans Andersen's fairy tales in China, many of his famous stories have undergone considerable transformation. From the above discussion, it can be concluded that the political appropriation of Andersen's works in a Chinese context is a product of the shifting political atmosphere in China. It demonstrates different political needs to exercise ideological manipulation. As the world continues to change, the refashioning of Andersen's tales, be it political or cultural or historical, will never stop.

Fantasy, Irony, and Autonomy
A Feminist Transcoding of "The Little Mermaid"

Wang Aiping
Associate Professor, Research Fellow of the Nordic
Literature Research Institute, Fudan University

The Transcodability of Andersen

Hans Christian Andersen studies in the national and international academic world have long been locked on the focal importance of his texts and their centrifugal receptions. Apart from textual study in the close-reading manner, contextual study which accommodates Andersen's works in the social, historical milieu concerned, inter-textual study which shapes/reshapes Andersen's meanings with reference to other (adapted) texts, and pre-textual study in the style of documentation to certify and verify the birth and growth of his works, there is a growing call for a more feasible post-textual approach in facilitating a healthy assimilation of Andersen's significance, so as to prevent rampant alienation otherwise resulting from the globalization process.

The post-textual study, in its better service to the Andersen heritage, adopts a more globalized and galvanized approach with the prime purpose of reaching a critical outlook and research methodology. Instead of regarding fidelity and translatability of Andersen's works as the main academic concern, the post-textual approach gives priority to universality and transcodability.

Analogous to the direct digital-to-digital conversion, a transcoding of Andersen works involves a decoding of the original data into a raw intermediate format and then re-encoding this into the target format. What comes to the fore is the core difference between a mere translating (or adapting) work and a transcoding work, that is, the creating of a raw intermediate format. This intermediate format is a highly essential and quintessential extract of the original verbal splendour of Andersen, which starts with a local expression (Denmark, Nordic) but ends with a global explanation and further aims at another localized extension (China).

The transcodability of Andersen is potentially great in its necessity and feasibility within the feminist critical context. Out of three cardinal feminist subjects, discourse, other than desire and domination, seems to be the most suitable springboard for the cracking and transmitting of the sense and sentience of the Andersen code based on the simple fact that many feminist writers and critics squarely claim fairy tales as their lives and particularly, their language which "dichotomizes people into the favoured and the unfavoured" (Walker 39).

In "The Little Mermaid", a prototypical example, Andersen presents a dichotomized world with a dominant androcentric and phallocentric power along with, or more exactly, opposed to an abused and silenced female world. The world the little mermaid inhabits epitomizes a pre-feminist structure at the centre of which stands the castle of the merking. He projects as well as personifies a set of interdictions that exert circumscriptive and prohibitive power over the mermaids (not the mermen). The mermaids are not allowed to swim to the surface of the sea until they are fifteen; they cannot weep or that will make their suffering even deeper and greater; they don't dare to dress themselves in the way they like for the only reason that "one has to suffer for position" (61); they have no mother to help sustain the maternal link in counterbalancing the paternal influence. Worse than that, the little mermaids have no names of their own, but are merely numbers (the first, the second..., the youngest). The letting go of her voice on the part of the little (the youngest) mermaid becomes the necessary condition for the love relationship with the prince. And this first metamorphosic act is followed by another one – the changing of the fishtail into human legs, which literally and symbolically indicates the violence and the price for the mermaid (women at large) to enter into a love (philosophical) discourse with the prince (male counterparts). The human world on the land is underpinned by an even harsher dichotomization because females are not only marginalized but even enslaved into currying favour with the prince in the familiar, courtly beer-and-skittles scenes.

If the tale of the little mermaid lays bare such an unequivocal and categorical logocentric discourse that determines the familial model, the conjugal model, or even the existential model, then the close study of the discourse activity and performativity of the little mermaid takes on a crying need and overriding importance in transcoding the feminist sense and sentience of Andersen texts.

The metamorphosis and the metaphysics of the little mermaid are unfolded by means of three developmental stages, at each of which the little mermaid is presented in her sea image, human image and aerial image respectively. To study how the little mermaid is spaced with (i.e. placed in the same space as) women (her siblings and her grandmother) in the beginning, with men (the prince and his men in the court) in the middle and with herself in the end, we can actually infer and interpret a dynamic discourse policy that the little mermaid adopts. And in her quest for the much-sought new womanhood, we can further generate a transcodable and archetypal pattern, namely, the little mermaid's, or rather, women's hard-earned discourse strategies: fantasy, irony, and autonomy.

Fantasy, an Oppositional Alternative

Modern fantasy, with fairytale fantasy as its subgenre, has long been functioning as a complicated mass dream-life in the most wide-awake society. The subtle relationship between fantasy and reality is both dynamic and dialectic as argued by Marcia Westkott:

> Fantasy not only opposes real conditions, but also reflects them. The opposition that fantasy expresses is not abstract, but is rooted in the real conditions themselves, in concrete social relations. As a negation, fantasy suggests an alternative to these concrete conditions. (Habegger 7)

From the fantasy-reality perspective, "The Little Mermaid" of Andersen can be regarded as a literary critique of the existing norms and structures informed by as well as based on the misogynist traditions and stereotypical assumptions about women's identity and sexuality. In refusing to be materialized in an essentialist and binary notion of what women are and are supposed to be, the little mermaid starts to harbour variants of fantasy, dreams or daydreams of transgressing the boundaries between mermaids and human beings, of crossing the lines between mer-maids (female) and hu-mans (male), which become subversive ways of overcoming relegation and marginalization in pursuit of female autonomy and authority.

In their initial break from their assigned femininity and enclosed domesticity, women turn their interest and invest their passion in a feminist alternative: nurturing and embracing a new womanhood.

When Andersen says that the little mermaid likes "nothing better than to listen to [the] old grandmother tell about the world above" (58)[1] and "[there is] so much that she [wants] to know" (65), we delightedly catches sight of an anxious and ambitious young lass who is on the same spiritual wavelength with mythically reputed amazons while being at variance with strict conformity and stringent conventionality in her immediate milieu. In sharp contrast to her dark little garden, the first impression of the human world the little mermaid gets is irresistibly fascinating. "The sun [has] just set. The clouds still [have] the colour of roses and on the horizon [is] a fine line of gold; in the pale pink sky the first star of evening [sparkles], clearly and beautifully." (62). Naturally, her wish to quit her sea clan for the as yet unknown world of the land motivates as well as endorses a self-esteeming and self-redeeming Bildungsroman, the most familiar feminist trope for inner experience, an inner experience marked by an unswerving embarcation on and an epic fight for the difference of identity and the identity of difference.

If what motivates the little mermaid's adventure is her dauntless imagination of an alternative sense and sentience of selfhood, then what sustains this formidable adventure is a bond of sisterhood, held dear by Showalter as "a Female Aesthetic" or "a politics of feminist survival" (146). In feminist fantasies, there are always sporadic but didactic chances for women to engage in their intra-dependent and inter-dependent world that help to sharpen their aspiration, live up their lives, and toughen their resolve.

One remarkable hallmark of such a bond of spiritual affinity and sympathy is the women's talk. While women's talk, not infrequently termed as chitchat for its light and gossipy nature, is conveniently downgraded as trivial and superficial in the broadbrush treatment of most male writers, Andersen gives a blow-by-blow account of the mermaids' talk, especially and exclusively about what the life on the land, fantasised as an alternative to their grim reality, is and means to them. Thanks to the exceptionally lavish effort of Andersen, the six mermaids, each respectively with a verbatim report in a solid length of a paragraph, can "have hundreds of things to tell" (59) and to share. And we readers can glean some rare moments of their burning

---

[1] Throughout this paper and concerning Andersen tales, I quote from *The Complete Fairy Tales and Stories*. Trans. Erik Christian Haugaard. Doubleday, New York, 1974.

curiosity, whimsical fantasy and inflamed avidity, rare because they are habitually silent and inarticulate. So, "many evenings [the little mermaids] would take each other's hands and rise up through the waters. They had voices far lovelier than any human beings." (61). The jointly woven and beautifully voiced dream is not so much narratively indispensable as symbolically laudable. Being more spoken to than speaking up, the little mermaids are especially meritorious when their fantastic constructing of a brand-new alternative is paramount to the birth of their brand-new womanhood. Later when puzzled by questions like if she can "do anything to win an immortal soul" (66), the little mermaid immediately goes to her grandmother, in unmistaken defiance of such well-established authority as her father/king while resorting to the silver cord (here the grandmother is playing the role of the absent mother). Undoubtedly, it is this congenital and cohesive bond of female intelligence and allegiance the little mermaid cherishes with her siblings and her grand-maternal guru that really helps her to endure the physical and spiritual throes and trials later.

By being 'speaking women (even to themselves)', by 'speaking about women', and by having 'women speaking to women', the little mermaids (women) achieve their linguistically constructed subjectivity in lieu of their former stigmatic passivity, delightedly patronized by their own kind and radically revolutionized in their aesthetic politics. That is the reason why "The Little Mermaid" is read as such a fantasy that it is not some "febrile phantasmagoria but an energetic dramatization of a better future" (Habegger 8) linking up with something collective and communal. It can also be celebrated as a breakthrough in the same marrow of the feminist utopia where gender power imbalances could be obliterated simply by throwing into sharp relief either a single-sex world or a genderless enclave.

There are times, undeniably, when the little mermaid's out-of-box thought and more-than-usual audacity are regarded as foolhardy. Her grandmother wants to dispel her attachment to the human world by the down-to-earth happiness they are enjoying. "We live far happier down here than man does up there." (66). The sea witch simply threatens her with a hazardous trip of no return. "[The] first morning after [the prince] has married another, your heart will break and you will become foam on the ocean." (69). However, with a narrative consolidation and Andersenian perspective of the former experience of enclosure and exclusion of the little mermaids (women in general), her wish to transcend boundaries and bondages should be judged as positive as Patricia Meyer Spacks explains:

> The idea that women may find their most significant freedom through fantasy or imagination need not imply any commitment to madness. Saner visions of the imagination as salvation [...] substantiate the possibility that the liberated inner life may create new freedoms of actual experience. (402)

When the little mermaid is so immersed in her fantasy-come-true relationship with reality that she can run the risk of being de-tailed (deprived of her tail), she can also pass a number of tests composed of both aspirations and distortions or transformation and finally emerge as whole and heroic. Andersen's fairytale fantasy underscores the dire need and full potential of female images of change and empowerment rather than stasis and entrapment structured by an appositional – male – position.

Irony, towards the Absolute Negativity

If fantasy characteristically counterpoints "the unsaid and the unseen of culture: that which had been silenced, made invisible, covered over and made 'absent'" (Jackson 3-4) and pinpoints the hegemonism in the current discourse which Andersen girls find impossible to appropriate, then irony is the language mode they adopt when they brave their passage right into the men's world, only to be confronted with female Quixotism.

There is no verbal irony in "The Little Mermaid" because the little mermaid is already dumb before she goes to the prince's court. But dramatic irony is prepared far ahead in the scene at the "turbulent maelstrom" (67) where the little mermaid exchanges her beautiful voice for the magic draught concocted by the sea witch who says, "[B]ut that voice you will have to give to me. I want the most precious thing you have to pay for my potion." (69). So far, Andersen has established a means of complicity between us readers and himself, as we are rightly informed of the definite loss of the love's labour whereas the innocent little mermaid is not. The installation (the first stage) of this dramatic irony is laid out in a mere slash off of the mermaid's tongue without let and hindrance and the suspension (the second stage) of this dramatic irony is also cut short in a mere transitional sentence: "Day by day the prince [grows] fonder and fonder of her; but he [loves] her as he would have loved a good child, and [has] no thought of making her his queen." (71). This love crisis, amply predictable, is nowhere near a solution/resolution (the final stage of dramatic irony) simply because situational irony already sets in and soon takes hold of the whole situation.

"Situational irony, [...] most broadly defined as a situation where the outcome is incongruous with what was expected" (Elleström 51) renders the little mermaid a female Quixote[2] bogged down in the foiled marriage plot. In a formulaic story with the marriage plot, the heroine is supposed to endure privation, excruciation or even humiliation before she finally receives the bliss of a happy wedlock. But there is no "happily-ever-after" mode of nuptial payoff and cathartic abreaction in the case of the little mermaid, which is to our expectation rather than our dismay. Andersen, the ironist, by giving the lie to a number of the myths that women are inculcated to believe with the efficacy of the marriage plot as one of them, relates and orients the individual female conjugal model to an institution of a patriarchal schema, hence the tragic inevitability.

The first handicap in the conjugal potential of the little mermaid is her lack of a name. As "the youngest mermaid" (58) in her father's castle, or "his little foundling" (71) in the prince's court, she becomes the second-to-none mouthpiece of a gender without named identities of their own. And being unnamed and unmarked is not far from being unvoiced. Symbolic of the silencing of women is the narrative fact that her letting go of her voice is a prerequisite as well as a price tag for a man-woman relationship. Far too traumatized by this involuntary sacrifice, she only vaguely asks herself, "What will I have left?" (69). The consequence is, of course, too severe to be bearable, severe not only in the physical sense but more in the moral sense, for when the story of life-saving cannot be proven, she can find nothing left for her to corroborate her virtuously deserved marriageability. She can only "capture a man's heart" by her "beautiful body, graceful walk, and lovely eyes" (69) instead of winning a man's heart by a deed of merit.

A nameless, voiceless and, naturally, virtueless little mermaid is not enough for Andersen to depict an essential plight of a female Quixote.

---

2 The term comes from *The Female Quixote* by Charlotte Lennox published in 1752.

The first meeting of the prince and the little mermaid now in human shape is cast in a familiar freeze-frame as well as an asymmetrical power framework characterized by that crippling "male gaze".[3] "He [looks] at her with his coal-black eyes. She [looks] downward." (70). To the second-wave feminists, this abusive and aggressive kind of gaze constitutes a neat superiority-vs.-inferiority binary opposition, expeditiously reinforcing the power of the male gazer and simultaneously undermining the power of the gazed by reducing the female recipient to an object. The downcast look of the little mermaid reveals a passive internalization of the phallocentric norms as well as a negative penalization of her erotic body. "She [is] naked; and therefore she [takes] her long hair and [covers] herself with it." (70). The letting go of her self-esteem and the letting in of her self-abasement, especially her feeling uneasy and inhibited about her nudity when under male surveillance typifies an objectified woman subject to the prevalent privilege of seeing with the male I/eye and showcases a wrenching and distressing process of incapacitation and traumatization. The little mermaid has never been seen, since then, as dauntless and boundless as she is initially determined to handle her own fate.

Admittedly, this loss of spiritual authority largely comes from a lack of physical authenticity, footnoted by the metamorphosic experience of the little mermaid from a sea creature to a human body. The de-tailing (getting rid of her fishtail) of herself in quest of a pair of human legs incurs the somatic pang as "every step [feels] as though she were walking on sharp knives" (70). Worse than that, it also triggers a spiritual mayhem. When a woman is defined by what she lacks instead of what she possesses and how she differs, by what she is not instead of what she is and could be, she is not only othered but also dehumanized. Irony turns to be more poignant and pungent when this otheredness goes beyond a redline limit: The human little mermaid is not even taken as a woman when the prince "[has] man's clothes made for her, so that she [can] accompany him when he [goes] horseback riding" (71).

Irony of different kinds reveals that the male-dominated language together with the world that this arbitrary language describes and circumscribes is fundamentally untrustworthy, i.e. it can be constructed

---

3   The concept was popularized in Laura Mulvey's essay "Visual Pleasure and Narrative Cinema" (1973).

(more exactly, manipulated) and can lie, as women have been constructed, manipulated and lied to. This language is also counterproductive, i.e. it is handicapping to "*l'ecriture feminine*", the much sought-after inscription of the autonomous female body.[4] Andersen's little mermaid employs some forms of irony in her human-world experience in order to either make fun of the hu-man (men's) validity in language or to undermine the authority of a language regime with the exclusion of mer-maids (women). When feminists regard the personal as political, it is usually this praiseworthy challenge to the linguistically hierarchical absoluteness that carries weight and might. Only, martyred women have suffered too much for this inconvenient truth. Undeservedly so.

Autonomy, a Utopian Modality

To feminists, *l'ecriture feminine* means coming to terms with inner disturbance while still maintaining sanity. Feminist utopia is just a sober and sensible negotiation between the familiar and the alien, the familiar (the conventional) being the "father's castle" (61) while the alien (the sought-after) being "a room of one's own".[5] However, when women cannot own rooms of their own, much less themselves, utopian writing forks into "the critical utopia" and "the critical dystopia" (Baccolini 16-17).

In some senses, "The Little Mermaid" is dystopian if the little mermaid could never talk again to tell (write) her own story. When the prince says "I must go, I must look at the beautiful princess" (72) (subtextually, 'I' as the condescending patron), when the little mermaid "dances and laughs with the thought of death in her heart" (74) (the familiar grin-and-bear-it cast of mind), when the news of the prince's wedding comes and makes the little mermaid think "of all she [has] lost in this world" (74) (self-deprecation behavioural code), Andersen seems to imply women's frailty and inferiority, not necessarily innate but socially constructed with that patriarchal order and totalitarian

---

4   "Women's writing" is coined by feminist theorist Hélène Cixous in her essay "The Laugh of the Medusa" (1975), where she asserts "Woman must write herself: must write about women and bring women to writing, from which they have been driven away as violently as from their bodies."

5   This is the title of an essay by Virginia Woolf based on a series of lectures she delivered at Newnham College and Girton College, two women's colleges at Cambridge University, in October 1928.

discourse at the back. Nothing seems more dishearteningly appropriate than the muffled expression of the little mermaid's vain struggle and resistance in Andersen's depiction: "The little mermaid's hand [trembles] as it squeezes the handle of the knife, and then she [throws] the weapon out into the sea." (75).

However, Andersenian tales about women as oppositional texts will not let amazon-likened little mermaids lie passive and submissive. To our relief, there is a new genre, according to some literary critics, that negates "the notions of utopia and dystopia as mutually exclusive terms" (Baccolini 18), by either setting up "utopian enclaves within the larger dystopian world", or maintaining utopia "in dystopia only outside the story" (Baccolini 18). In the end, we see the utopian light shine through with all its gospel revelation about resurrection and redemption.

> The sun [rises] out of the sea; its rays [feel] warm and soft on the deathly cold foam. But the Little mermaid [does] not feel death, she [sees] the sun, and up above her [float] hundreds of airy, transparent forms [...]. (75)

The resurrection of the little mermaid is achieved intriguingly through a revived life by assuming a new metamorphosic shape. "The little mermaid [looks] down and [sees] that she [has] an ethereal body." (75). When some critics think that the third role of the little mermaid in the form of an air creature is a far-fetched fig leaf, an after-witted redresser or a dangerous superfluity in explaining away a deeply ingrained male oppression, some are more than willing to take it as a significant follow-through to save the little mermaid's "sexual/textual politics"[6] from being mired and stranded. If Andersen makes the little mermaid the first billing of the tale instead of one of the second sex, and if Andersen makes the little mermaid a brave female model instead of one of the fair sex, he must find an Archimedian fulcrum to elevate the conception. This pivoting point is the female body with or without its transmutations.

Indeed, feminists regard the female body as the sight of power while power is a central concept in their literary criticism, as Joan Scott has maintained, "gender is a primary field within which or by means of

---

[6] The expression comes from Toril Moi's *Sexual/Textual Politics: Feminist Literary Theory* published in 1985.

which power is articulated" (Allen 1). In studying the form and transformation, expression and distortion of the female body, feminists can drive home some harsh facts and concomitant annealing instructions by means of "understanding, criticizing, challenging, subverting and ultimately overturning the multiple axes of stratification affecting women" (Allen 2).

The metamorphosis of the little mermaid from the cursed fishtail to the inauthentic human legs showcases a full body of feminist metaphysics on corporeality and identity. The little mermaid becomes acquainted with one of such axes of stratification, that is, women are the objects of men's desire, from the old merwoman who seems to be very conversant in that. "Only if a man should fall so much in love with you, [...] then his soul would flow into your body and you would be able to partake of human happiness." (66). In this well-accepted image of women as a sexual receptacle, there is no space for female initiative and inventive selfhood. Only by fitting themselves squarely into the entrenched gender grooves and by toeing the line with the solid and hard power type (embodied and reiterated in "the marble statue of a boy" (58) in the garden of the little mermaid and a prince who is like the marble statue) could they finally enter into the love discourse with men. Another axis of stratification concerns women's unalterable and unalienable duty in "[capturing] a human heart" (70) by their erotic body, which determines the materialistic nature of a man-woman relationship and which denies a spiritual fulfilment for women. Still, putting the female body, especially the nude one, under censorial and censorious male surveillance is another self-justified and highly-institutionalized stratification. When the female body turns out to be a pitfall for female entrapment, then a final breaking free from this corporeal shackle is both formidable and laudable. Salient and explicit is Andersen's eagerness to marvel at this self-liberation and self-empowerment by letting the little mermaid change into a form "so fragile and fine that no human eye could see [it]" (75), with the human eye standing for sexual vulgarity and political conformity.

The redemption of the little mermaid is more inspirational than her resurrected corporeal identity, inspirational in the sense that this "[daughter] of the air" (75) has resumed her long lost voice which is none other than the carrier of her hard-earned autonomy. As we can imagine, her voice is so "melodious, so spiritual and tender that no human ear could hear [it]" (75), with human ear standing for the discriminating and silencing force. Coming back together with the voice is the moral payoff and immortal prospect. "You have suffered and borne your suffering bravely; and that is why you are among us, the spirits of the air." (76). The feminist merits of hardship-bearing and dream-nurturing are not much appreciated let alone rewarded in the dystopian world down on the human land but are rightly deserved in the utopian paradise. When the little mermaid thinks, "Do *my* good deeds and in three hundred years an immortal soul will be *mine*" and "*I* shall rise like this into God's kingdom" (76; italics are mine), Andersen is more than willing to present the long pent-up vision of the immortality which is all the more rewarding for those who not only treat their bodies as symbols of sovereignty but also as agents of self-empowerment. "Mermaids have no immortal soul and can never have one, unless they can obtain the love of a human being. Their chance of obtaining eternal life depends upon others. We daughters of the air have not *received* an eternal soul either; but we can *win* one by good deeds." (76; italics are mine). This carefully phrased difference from "receive" to "win" based on a comparison between the sea and human image to the aerial image of the little mermaid champions an affirmative autonomous sexual/political strategy in accordance with which the little mermaid has her authorship and mastership in her own hand and by her own virtues.

In this sense, "The Little Mermaid" is a feminist text resonant with utopian modality, morality, and immortality.

The Death of the Immortal Andersen

In the spirit of the post-structuralist "death of the author",[7] every reading (transcoding) strongly rewrites a text. A book could have (a) different author(s), hence becoming (a) different book(s). The belief that books write authors symbolizes the deauthorization or simply the death of the author.

But if we put a positive spin on Barthes' claim, we are glad to see that transcoding Andersen's works, say, "The Little Mermaid", though has rendered Andersen more obscure yet bringing more significance to Andersen studies. The significance lies in converting Andersen's

---

7 This is the title of the 1967 essay by Roland Barthes collected in *Image, Music, Text* (1977).

individual text into a social text which valorizes and popularizes Andersenian feminist sense and sentience.

The feminist discourse code in the "The Little Mermaid" – fantasy, irony, and autonomy – presents a critical paradigm in the study of female enterprise and metaphysical rise in the quest of their substantial identity and existential validity. Fantasy is the locus of an idealized construction of feminist awareness in opposition to the phallocentric structure and its vested interests. Irony denotes a head-on clash between what is socially/culturally hegemonic and the physically/spiritually dispossessed, leading to the pathetic victimization and traumatization of the female. Autonomy serves to add celebratory, jubilant touch with a moral award to those who have masculinized through the asymmetrical power relation and concomitantly, with a spiritual epiphany over immortal human (humanitarian) values.

A further study of fantasy, irony and autonomy also helps to strike a paradoxical note in this feminist critical paradigm. A fantasy could be as concrete and real as the tangible facts of life. Discourse power is both silencing and liberating, depending on who is in possession of it. A pursuit for equal rights should be fulfilled through 'differed' experience. True triumph in the feminist incarnation could well be achieved by means of non-corporeality.

When this decoded paradigm looms larger and larger with its convincing core values and exemplary role models, readers can go closer and closer to Andersen while further and further away from his mere authorship because they are enabled to encode/reencode feminist sense and sentience into (a) text(s) of their own out of a glocalized (global-local) background.

In assigning a homework on rewriting the story of "The Little Mermaid" to a class of sophomore students, the author of this essay is delighted to see the majority of the students (mostly female) keep the gist in the "fantasy" and "autonomy" parts but perform a mercilessly critical operation on the middle-course of "irony", while almost all male students are only too ready to accept the ready-made fate of the little mermaid. When male students justify that immortality is already the best compensation for the little mermaid, their female counterparts place an emphasis on a self-motivated and hard-earned happiness for the little mermaid to endorse her autonomous spirit. By finding the crux as early as in the proverbial pacts with the devil, girl students regard such Faustian bargain as being diabolically ill-meant and strategically short-sighted (often exchanging a long cherished soul for a short term gain). In their ideological imagination and narrative remedy, the little mermaid outsmarts the sea witch so that she still keeps the fishtail and retains the beautiful voice because the body and the voice are the belt and braces of her feminist identity and by means of which she can successfully remind the prince of the life-and-death bond between them. There is no worry about the barrier of whatever kind between a sea creature and a human being for the love potion (a relation on an equal basis) instead of the witch's potion (a relation of bondage demanding sacrifice) finally turns the little mermaid into a human figure as a result of sublimation to avoid an otherwise desperate immolation. And they live happily hereafter.

Thus conceived, transcoding Andersenian feminist sense and sentience in a post-textual style is, in its true nature, critically intertextualizing between an androtext and a gynotext, between a pre-feminist mindset and a postmodern type and perchance between a Nordic writer and a Chinese student. Given that this trans-historical, trans-continental and trans-cultural intertextuality can liberate and proliferate the feminist profundity and applicability in our textual and social milieu, our Chinese students and scholars feel it incumbent on ourselves to unfailingly evaluate, elevate and disseminate the metaphysical insight and the spiritual delight of a little mermaid.

Hans Christian Andersen and the Arabesque

Jacob Bøggild
Professor, the Hans Christian Andersen Center,
University of Southern Denmark

As one can learn from various contributions to this book, the duration and depth of the Chinese reception of Hans Christian Andersen has been nothing short of remarkable. This indicates that there must be certain features of Chinese culture definitely dating a considerable way back in history which have made – and still make – China especially receptive to Andersen's literary universe. One literary phenomenon, amongst what must be quite a few others, which *perhaps* could help illuminate some such features, could be that of the arabesque. But it would be too difficult to pursue that complex question in this context.

Instead, I will suggest a perspective from which Hans Christian Andersen's fairy tales and stories can be comprehended as an interconnected whole – a genuine unity – and not just as an assembly of texts that happen to be written by the same writer and of course bear witness to that fact in various ways. And I will suggest that it is indeed the literary arabesque which can provide the perspective just mentioned. But the arabesque was not a literary mode – it is not a genre, but a mode – to begin with, and many people might not at all suppose it to have anything to do with literature. Therefore, I would like to start by outlining a small trajectory of the arabesque.

As the name indicates, the arabesque was originally connected to Arabian culture – although something similar to the mode of the arabesque was also employed in Hellenism. The strict iconoclasm of Islam made it necessary to develop an abstract form of decorative art and the arabesque was on hand to meet this demand. Often, arabesque decorations would take the shape of plant-like ornaments.

The mode of the arabesque as a form of decoration entered Western culture through several stages. The last of them was the Moorish presence in Spain and Portugal. The arabesque mode of decoration flourished in the periods of the Baroque and the Rococo. At first, this mode was mainly used for the decoration of frames and the like, but gradually the arabesque – in accordance with its potentially infinite nature – entered and came to dominate the framed space as well. From the point of view of Classicism, which succeeded the Baroque and Rococo periods, this kind of overflowing ornamentation was superfluous, destabilising and therefore – at least in the opinion of some classicists – even immoral.

The figurehead of the early Romantic breakthrough in Germany was Friedrich Schlegel (1772-1829). The task he set himself was to write the agendas and manifestoes of this new movement. And he performed a clever polemical move when he, notably in his "Brief über den Roman" (Letter on the Novel) from 1800, made the arabesque a central watchword when writing these agendas and manifestoes, thereby precisely turning it into a literary concept or category. In this way, he effectively contrasted the new Romantic poetics with classicist poetics. Intriguingly, in this context, Schlegel was in fact, amongst a whole range of other things, an orientalist. He was, however, not a sinologist, but mostly read old Indian texts. He could read Sanskrit fluently.

Schlegel's Romantic literary arabesque is an artfully arranged disorder which mimics the productive human imagination: a mixing of opposites full of tension and potential as well as a mixing of styles and genres. Let me just note in passing that artfully arranged disorder, a predilection for the imagination, the mixing of opposites, and the mixing of genres and styles, are all highly applicable when characterizing Andersen's fairy tales and stories as a whole.

The original nature of the arabesque as abstract ornamentation, however, is still very much preserved even when it is transformed into a literary mode. Many of the Romantics regarded the most abstract art form, music, as the highest one and therefore to them music was the ideal to which the arabesque literary work should strive to approximate as much as possible. Music can lend a voice to moods and emotions that cannot be captured or expressed by means of words and in this way music in a way becomes the upper and nether limit of language – and by extension literature. The basic musical elements of words, rhythm and tone, can be condensed into meaningful utterances – and meaning, of course, can in turn be dissolved into song. Let me, again in passing, note that the musical quality of Andersen's prose is significant in some of his fairy tales, and very much so in his stories and his travel books.

According to Schlegel, the novel is the ultimate arabesque genre, precisely because it accommodates the mixing of all other genres. But the fairy tale, the genre of human imagination par excellence, and the prose sketch are also arabesque literary forms. The prose sketch is an arabesque form because, as outline and abstraction, it considerably appeals to the co-productive imagination of the reader.

Having given this rough outline of the trajectory arabesque, I wish to turn to Andersen in more detail and begin zooming in on his arabesque poetics. That there is an arabesque aspect to Andersen's writing has been acknowledged before. It was pointed out by himself and others when he was still alive, and it has become a topic in some recent Andersen-research.

The first of Andersen's works which was recognized as an arabesque was his fantastic rhapsody *Journey on Foot* (*Fodreise fra Holmens Canal til Østpynten af Amager i Aarene 1828-29*) from 1829, a work which marked his first breakthrough as a writer, albeit only locally – in Copenhagen. The most influential critic in Copenhagen at that time, Johan Ludvig Heiberg, reviewed it favourably, though still somewhat condescendingly. Heiberg wrote about the young author that he:

"[...] is situated in approximately the same position as a painter, who, before he ventures to attempt more rigorous compositions, first practises painting in the mode of the arabesque; because in the arabesque, too, the various elements are random, heterogeneous and indifferent towards each other, whereas the originality and grace, by means of which they are fused, provide it with artistic value." (131)[1]

---

1   "Forfatteren befinder sig omtrent i samme Stilling, som en Maler, der inden han vover sig til strengere Compositioner, først øver sig paa Arabesken; thi ogsaa i Arabesken ere Elementerne tilfældige, heterogene og ligegyldige imod hverandre, men den Originalitet og den Gratie, hvormed de ere sammensmeltede, give den Kunstværd."
    All translations into English are mine. This also is the case when it comes to texts by Hans Christian Andersen. This quotation is translated from the edition of *Journey on Foot* (*Fodreise*) listed among the references at the end of the present book. Concerning the other Andersen texts in this paper, I quote from *Andersen. H. C. Andersens samlede værker*. 1-18. København: Gyldendal/Det danske Sprog- og Litteraturselskab, 2003-2007 (Collected Works of H. C. Andersen).

Randomness and heterogeneity are indeed prominent features of *Journey on Foot*. Later on, Andersen would himself refer to it as "a kind of fantastic arabesque". Another work, Andersen himself spoke of as an arabesque was *Picture Book without Pictures* (*Billedbog uden Billeder*, 1839).

Both works are characterized by the absence of an elaborate and coherent plot. *Journey on Foot* is a kind of fictitious travel book, where various fantastic tableaus succeed each other. *Picture Book without Pictures* consists of a series of prose sketches. Each sketch, allegedly, represents an episode that the moon has witnessed on its voyage round the earth and related to the narrator of the frame, who has then written it down for us to read. This is a very thin frame story, indeed.

Thus, there are similarities between these two works and Andersen's genuine travel books, where descriptions, episodes, and reflections are strung like pearls on a string.

However, the arabesque aspect of Andersen's writing gradually went out of focus, probably because the arabesque as a literary mode did, at least in Danish literary criticism and research. Recently, however, Niels Kofoed has brought this aspect of Andersen into focus again.[2] But Kofoed predominantly focuses on the texts that I have mentioned: *Journey on Foot*, *Picture Book without Pictures* and a couple of the travel books. Of Andersen's fairy tales and stories, it is only "Auntie Toothache" ("Tante tandpine", 1872), a very late tale which refers all the way back to one of the tableaus in *Journey on Foot*, which he considers to be arabesque to any significant degree.

In my view, Kofoed's perspective could – indeed must – be vastly expanded. As mentioned, I suggest that we conceive of Andersen's entire corpus of fairy tales and stories as one huge arabesque entity where the same motifs and themes are repeated again and again in new ways and often in contradictory terms.

In fact, a character in one of Andersen's novels, the Jewess Esther in *To Be or not to Be* (*At være eller ikke være*, 1857), delivers a brilliant characterization of the genre of the fairy tale as a genre which is fundamentally arabesque:

---

2   In the paper "The arabesque and the grotesque" and the monograph *Arabesken og dens æstetiske former* (The arabesque and its aesthetic forms).

> I find that fairy tales constitute the most extensive realm of poetry. This realm reaches from the blood-fuming graves of ancient times to the picture books of innocent, playful childhood. It engages folk literature as well as *Kunstmärchen*. To me, it represents all genuine poetry, and the one who masters it, must include in it the tragic, the comic, the naïve and irony and humour, and has in turn both the lyrical string, childlike narrating and the language of science at his service. (6, 244)³

In accordance with Schlegel's idea of the arabesque, the kind of fairy tale evoked here institutes a symmetrical yet tension-filled interaction between opposites: folk literature and artistic literature, tragedy and comedy, naivety and irony, the lyrical mode and childlike narrating.

Andersen's own fairy tales very much conform to this ideal. Georg Brandes (1842-1927), the most prominent Danish literary critic since Heiberg and an avatar of what we refer to as 'the modern breakthrough', was acutely aware of this fact, which the following passage from his portrait of Andersen as an author (1869) aptly demonstrates:

> The fairy tales add up to a whole, a radiating piece of weaving which appears to say to its beholder what the spider says in Aladdin [a drama by the Danish romantic poet Oehlenschläger, JB]: 'Behold my weak web, how the threads entangle!' [...] I would like to point out to the reader that he, in a famous work by Zeising, *Aesthetische Forschungen*, can see the whole series of opposing aesthetic concepts, with all their nuances [...] arranged like a great star, just like Andersen intended on the part of his fairy tales. (2, 123)⁴

---

3 "Jeg finder, at Eventyr-Digtningen er Poesiens meest vidt udstrakte Rige, det naaer fra Oldtids blodrygende Grave til den fromme barnlige Legendes Billedbog, optager i sig Folke-Digtningen og Kunst-Digtningen, det er mig Repræsentanten for al Poesie, og den, som mægter det, maa heri kunne lægge ind det Tragiske, det Komiske, det Naive, Ironien og Humoret, og har her baade den lyriske Streng, det Barnligtfortællende og Naturbeskriverens Sprog til sin Tjeneste [...]."

4 "Æventyrene danner et Hele, et i mangfoldige Radier udstraalende Væv, der synes at sige til Betragteren som Edderkoppen i Aladdin: "Betragt mit svage Spind, hvor Traadene sig flette!" [...] jeg [vil] gøre Læseren opmærksom paa, at han i et berømt videnskabeligt Værk af Zeising; *Aesthetische Forschungen*, vil kunne se den hele Række af æstetiske Modsætningsbegreber med alle deres nuancer [...] ordnede i en stor Stjerne, ganske som Andersen har tænkt sig det for sine Æventyrs Vedkommende."

According to Brandes, Andersen's grand plan with his fairy tales and stories is to arrange opposites in tension-filled, antithetic or contrapuntal ways.

The following passage from Brandes' portrait is even more stunning in the present context:

> While the fairy tales as a whole [...] are always united by an idea, this whole can, as regards the form, be compared to the fantastic, decorative paintings in which peculiarly stylized plants, lively flowers, doves, peacocks and human forms intertwine in interchanging ways. (2, 95-96)[5]

One might even discern a slight tinge of the grotesque in this illustration, if one considers the hybrid forms evoked.

In the light of Brandes' characterizations of the poetics of Andersen's fairy tales quoted here, it is odd indeed that when he at all mentions the arabesque in the portrait – and he only does that once – it is with a negative ring. He talks of "the confused arabesques of *Journey on Foot*". I think the reason for this fact is that Brandes was no friend of Romanticism and would be wary of writing anything that could be conceived as enrolling Andersen in that movement.

Allow me to cite my second quotation from Brandes again:

> While the fairy tales as a whole [...] are always united by an idea, this whole can, as regards the form, be compared to the fantastic, decorative paintings [...] in which peculiarly stylized plants, lively flowers, doves, peacocks and human forms intertwine in interchanging ways.

It is precisely the aesthetics of such paintings which Andersen describes – and applies – in a passage from the fairy tale "The Garden of Paradise" ("Paradisets Have", 1839). A prince arrives in this garden and the scenery which greets him is portrayed in this manner:

> Were these palm trees that grew there, or immense water plants? Such vast and verdant trees the Prince had never seen before. The most marvellous climbing vines hung in garlands such as are to be seen only in old

---

5 "Medens Æventyrdigtningen [...] saaledes altid holdes sammen af en Idé, kan den med hensyn til Form sammenlignes med de fantastiske Dekorationsmalerier [...], i hvilke ejendommeligt stiliserede Planter, livfulde Blomster, Duer, Paafugle og Menneskeskikkelser slynger sig sammen og gaar over i hverandre."

illuminated church books, painted in gold and bright colours in the margins or twined about the initial letters. Here were the oddest assemblages of birds, flowers and scrolls. On the grass near-by, with their brilliantly starred tails spread wide, was a flock of peacocks. Or so they seemed, but when the Prince touched them he found that these were not birds. They were plants. They were large burdock leaves that were as resplendent as a peacock's train. (1, 219)[6]

This is certainly a scenery of the grotesque and arabesque; we get strange assemblages of for example birds and flowers – we might even be mistaken as to which is which – and a tendency towards abstractions in the form of twists and twirls. Thus, the passage is inserted in "The Garden of Paradise" as a kind of arabesque watermark.

The inclusion of such watermarks is a common trait in the arabesque tradition in literature. A fine example can be found in E. T. A. Hoffmann's *Der Goldne Topf* (1814). Hoffmann (1776-1822) is one of the writers Andersen is most inspired by. The main character of *Der Goldne Topf* (The Golden Flower Pot), Anselmus, is provided with the task of copying manuscripts for an archivist, Lindhorst. Like the prince of "The Garden of Paradise" he is somewhat disoriented:

[...] Anselmus wondered a lot about the strangely interlacing letters, and the sight of the many points, lineaments, curves and scrolls, which seemed to form now plants, now mosses and now animal shapes, made his mood sink as to whether he could copy them correctly.[7]

The parallels between this passage and the one from "The Garden of Paradise" cannot be overlooked. In both instances, we find shapes of plants and animals as well as scrolls and a reference to written signs.

---

6 "Var det Palmetræer, eller kjæmpestore Vandplanter, her groede! saa saftige og store Træer havde Prindsen aldrig før seet; i lange Krandse hang der de forunderligste Slyngplanter, som de kun findes afbildede med Farver og Guld paa Randen af de gamle Helgenbøger eller snoe sig der gjennem Begyndelses-Bogstaverne. Det var de sælsomste Sammensætninger af Fugle, Blomster og Snørkler. I Græsset tæt ved stod en Flok Paafugle med udbredte straalende Haler! Jo det var rigtignok saa! nei da Prinsen rørte ved dem, mærkede han, at det ikke var Dyr, men Planter: det var de store Skrægger, der her straalede som Paafuglens deilige Hale."

7 "[...] Anselmus wunderte sich nicht wenig über die seltsam verschlungenen Zeichen, und bei dem Anblick der vielen Pünktchen, Striche und Züge und Schnörkel, die bald Pflanzen, bald Moose, bald Tiergestalten darzustellen schienen, wollte ihm beinahe der Mut sinken, alles so genau nachmalen zu können. Er geriet darüber in tiefe Gedanken."

I hope that I have succeeded in indicating that Hans Christian Andersen, like Hoffmann, writes in accordance with the arabesque tradition in Western Literature which was founded – or at least made an explicit tradition – by Friedrich Schlegel and his fellow early Romanticists in Germany. Here, alas, I have insufficient space to demonstrate how it is possible to conceive of Andersen's entire oeuvre of fairy tales and stories as one entire arabesque, but I can refer the reader to my monograph *Svævende stasis. Arabesk og allegori i H.C. Andersens eventyr og historier* (Gliding Stasis. Arabesque and Allegory in H.C. Andersen's Fairy Tales and Stories, 2012).

Instead, my final note in passing will be that in the traditional visual art of China one can also find a mixture or assemblage of stylized plants and birds and written signs. As I suggested to begin with, here might be something worth exploring as part of the wider exploration of the reasons for China's remarkable receptiveness to the universe of Hans Christian Andersen's fairy tales and stories.

Gender, Body, and Space
A Spatial Analysis of "The Little Mermaid"

Chen Liang
Associate Professor, Research Fellow of the Nordic
Literature Research Institute, Fudan University

Hans Christian Andersen's fairy tales are characterized by their rich expression of human affections, profound representation of humanity and novel design of plots. Briefly speaking, Chinese critics, in reviewing his works, have placed much emphasis on the tragic elements in the text, tracing the reason for the tragedy and its aesthetic features (Lan Shouting and Chen Ying 41). Also, since Hans Christian Andersen was much influenced by religion, the religious representation, in which love, original sin, and redemption are the central topics, has been heatedly discussed by Chinese critics. It is commonly believed that Andersen uses the form of fairy tales to express, disseminate and represent the notion of love shaped in Christianity (Qian Zhongli 100). In shaping his fairy tales, Andersen has absorbed many elements of folklore from native Danish culture and combined them with modern ideologies, which has attracted many Chinese scholars to explore the matrix and stereotypes in his texts, and what's more important, their modern transformation and reconstruction (Yang Ning 65). Besides the academic researches on his fairy tales, much translational work has been conducted.

Among his fairy tales, "The Little Mermaid" has been widely popular in Chinese criticism for the rich artistic and humanistic beauty of the heroine, the little mermaid. Many in-depth efforts have been made to explore the death ideology (Cheng Kaicheng and Ying Zhaohua 69), mythological stereotypes (Tang Jun and Yang Tianshu 88), and other topics. Yet, much room has also been left for further discussion. For example, how is female consciousness represented in the story? What is essential in its aesthetic mechanism? Is there any deep structure behind the conflicts and confrontations exhibited in the text? By applying spatial theory, which has never been undertaken before by Chinese scholars, the present study tries to investigate the spatial construction, power symbolization and body representation in the story in order to develop a new understanding of the theme and characters in the story as well as its aesthetic apprehension.

I

Space has become an indispensable perspective in humanistic perception of the world in modern Western contexts. It has originated from new cultural geology, combining both cultural geology and postmodern cultural theories. The ascendance of the importance of space is not only an academic discovery, but also the humanistic representation of the requirement of social practice and theoretical development.

Michel Foucault is one of the pioneering thinkers who has pointed out that the study of humanistic social science in the 20th century has turned from the perspective of temporality to spatiality. Later, in the construction of space theory, Henri Lefebvre has creatively developed the notion of "production" in Marxist philosophy. He holds that the significance of production is not confined to the dichotomy between subjectivity and objectivity, rather, it should be expanded to include spatial elements like body, means of production, as well as the interrelationship among the materials in a certain space. In *The Production of Space* (1974), Lefebvre holds that space can be categorized into three kinds: material, spiritual, and social. Before the appearance of comprehensive spatial theory, the three kinds of space were isolated and sporadic. The emergence of spatial theory organically combined the three spaces into a cubical being where the subjectivity in the space is much highlighted. Among the three spatial suppositions, the social space theory Henri Lefebvre put forth is the most influential, emphasizing that social space is produced by society, while at the same time it produces society. This theory has played a significant guiding role in the later development of space theory.

Based on Lefebvre's theory, Edward Soja has updated Lefebvre's concept of the spatial triad with his own concept of spatial trialectics which includes the third space, or spaces that are both real and imagined. The first space can be viewed as a specific materialistic form, which can be labelled, analysed and explained; while the second is also a spiritual construction of social existence. The third space transcends the previous two spaces and is more inclusive and open. Its significance lies in its review of the first and second spaces and the de-/reconstruction of them, which, by reevaluating the dichotomy between the first and second spaces, opens a new path to a space model.

Contemporary Western space theory has endowed space with independent subjectivity and equal status with time. Also, the theory highlights the complexity of various elements inside space which in turn exhibits the rich mechanism of the operation of space. This reform updates the traditional time-based perspective into a trinity notion which combines space, time, and existence. When applied to literary works, the space perspective may effectively exhibit some hidden textual features such as the subjectivity of characters, the relation between characters and environment and operative mechanisms of power. The continuous development of space theory has provided many insightful perspectives to writings and literary criticism. It helps to explore the text and investigate the environment in the text, the relationship between characters and space, narrative techniques and symbolic meaning in the space description, which have endowed literary criticism with original perspectives and help to discover new textual meaning and value in terms of writing techniques, structure, characterization, etc.

II

The present paper aims to approach "The Little Mermaid" from a spatial perspective and explore the text on two levels: the spatial coding and body representation in gender power; and the organic connection between space and body, between spatial change and plot development, in order to reveal the application of spatial mechanisms in the text and the role space plays in theme-shaping. From a spatial perspective, it can be observed that in the depiction of the fairytale world, Hans Christian Andersen completed the portrait of characters and shaping of thematic meaning through the spatial construction in the works. In his fairy tales, space does not only constitute the place where meaning comes into shape and plot develops but also embodies organic connections to the characters' personality, the plot development and the symbolic interpretation, etc. In addition, the construction of the outer space usually corresponds to the inner emotional changes and physical transformation of the characters, which constitutes the aesthetic peculiarity of "The Little Mermaid."

Generally speaking, in the textual space created by Andersen, a multi-layered space is constructed with much emphasis being placed on the inner mechanism of each specific space. During the construction of each specific space, Andersen, while following the traditional writing style in describing the materialistic existence of space, has enriched space with a powerful metaphoric function and turned it into a dynamic entity which reflects a social ideology of gender and power.

Specifically speaking, there are three spaces in "The Little Mermaid": the sea, the land, and the sky, which not only constitute the existential locations for the characters, but also reveal different subjectivities in respective space-layers. The process of the spatial transcending of the little mermaid from the bottom space of the sea to the top space of the sky is also the process of her spiritual purification. Space is not only a specific material framework but also spiritual reflection of the characters in the story.

The First Space: A Materialistic Space under Female Hegemony
The first space, that of the sea, Andersen has populated with many power signifiers defined by Foucault, e.g., the use of objective symbols to represent the coding mechanism in the female power structure. At the same time, he puts much emphasis on depicting the materialistic nature of this space.

In the textual description, the space in the sea is peculiarly exotic in terms of its marine features:

> The most marvelous trees and flowers grow down there, with such pliant stalks and leaves that the least stir in the water makes them move about as though they were alive. (67).[1]

The peculiar marine scene is not a simple exotic setting in the text; rather, it symbolizes the power mechanism in the vast marine space. The objects in the marine space are utilized to systematically exhibit the operation and controlling mechanism of the power system in the sea. Also, Andersen endows the spatial power with gender characteristics and, thus, gender power has become an important part of the spatial mechanism in "The Little Mermaid", and plays an essential role in creating textual meaning and characterization.

---

1   I quote from *Fairy Tales*, trans. Tiina Nunally. New York: Penguin Books, 2004.

In the sea space, most of the inhabitants are female. Besides, the figure which has the ultimate control over the sea space is the mother of the Sea King, even the marginalized figure, the witch, is a female too. The only male figure in the space is the Sea King, a subordinate who possesses no power and is speechless all the time. It can be safely concluded that the first sea space is a powerful female space which exerts control over the individual spaces and body constraints.

This control takes effect on all the mermaids who are confined in the chauvinistic space. The supervision extends from the management of their bodies to the manipulation over their own spaces and consciousness of identity. The mermaids do not have individual names, and are mentioned only numerically. "Each of the young princesses had a little plot of ground in the garden, where she might dig and plant as she pleased" (68). Although they have their own spaces, the spaces, as part of the whole marine space, have to be in line with its supervision, which helps to regulate the mermaids' consciousness of identity.

The method works well. All the mermaids obey the order of the time to rise to the surface. Except for the little mermaid, all the sisters decorate their own spaces in line with the marine features. The decorations clearly show their obedience to the manipulative spatial power system.

> One arranged her flower-bed into the form of a whale; another thought it better to make hers like the figure of a little mermaid. (68)

Yet, unlike the other sisters, the little mermaid longs for the scene above the sea. Her desire is so strong that she removes the marine-featured decorations favoured by her sisters from her space and chooses decorations which are characterized by the space of the sky. Also, she puts a beautiful marble statue of a handsome boy in her space, which serves as an image of her spiritual pursuit symbolizing the driving force that enables her to ascend from the first space to the second one.

> She cared for nothing but her pretty red flowers, like the sun, excepting a beautiful marble statue. It was the representation of a handsome boy, carved out of pure white stone, which had fallen to the bottom of the sea from a wreck. (68)

Gender, Body, and Space

For the little mermaid, the sky space is the high level on which her spiritual pursuit and female consciousness rest. By this analogy, Andersen tries to highlight the hidden connection of the sky space and the spiritual transcending of the little mermaid in the beginning of the story.

Then, in the following depiction of the marine space, Andersen makes many analogies between the sea space and the sky space, which reinforce the organic interaction between the two. When describing the marine scene, he writes: "Fishes, both large and small, glide between the branches, as birds fly among the trees here upon land" (67-68). In the marine palace,

> The large amber windows were open, and the fish swam in, just as the swallows fly into our houses when we open the windows [...]. Over everything lay a peculiar blue radiance, as if it were surrounded by the air from above, through which the blue sky shone, instead of the dark depths of the sea. (68)

These analogies are not simply scenic similarities between the two spaces. They may be viewed to be an observation from the perspective of the little mermaid, which constitutes a psychological hint for the readers concerning plot development and the spatial transcending of the little mermaid.

Secondly, the operational mechanism of power in space can be further analysed through the connection between physical features and spatial transformation. In the depiction of the inner environment of the space, the objective materials, including bodies, symbolize the coding mechanism and individual status of the power structure.

In spatial theory, the body constitutes the centre of the space. The transformation of the space is best represented by the physical transformation. In "The Little Mermaid", direct connections between the body and space are easily found, and, what is more important, the transformation of space is well accompanied by the transformation of body shape. In the text, the body has become a metaphor, foregrounding the inner value and significance of the space she is in and constructing the presence of each space. One of the spatial features in "The Little Mermaid" is the dynamic spatial changes, which keep changing with the plot development. According to spatial theory, the change of space is not objective, geological, architectural in its nature, but a change which involves the transformation of its focus and center: the body. The change of the body is also one of space and vice versa (Xie Na 67). This theory is best exemplified by the physical transformation of the little mermaid.

In the beginning of the story, the mother of the Sea King is portrayed as "a very wise woman, and exceedingly proud of her high birth; on that account she wore twelve oysters on her tail; while others, also of high rank, were only allowed to wear six" (67). First, we may notice that in the marine space, the existence of body is also a spatial one and it is the primary target to be under control in the space. The manipulation over the subject usually starts with the control and shaping of the body. As the decoration in the marine space, the twelve oysters not only add charm and beauty to the old mother, but also symbolically exhibit and reinforce her status in the space. Similar coding functions of the marine decoration can also be found on the body of the little mermaid. The grandmother is very fond of the little mermaid. On the day when the little mermaid is going to rise to the ocean surface, "she placed a wreath of white lilies in her hair, and every flower leaf was half a pearl. Then the old lady ordered eight great oysters to attach themselves to the tail of the princess to show her high rank" (71). Compared with the other mermaids, the additional two oysters have the similar function of status exhibition and reinforcement in the power hierarchy. On the one hand, they are the symbols of the grandmother's affection for the little mermaid, while on the other hand, they contain a disciplinary force which binds and regulates the little mermaid and leaves her no choice but to obey.

In the beginning, the little mermaid lacks the courage to challenge the grandmother and remains passive. When she is courageous enough to visit the sea witch, she has her body changed and enters the second space. Yet, her physical change, basically speaking, is to meet the male standard of beauty, and hence her female beauty remains an object under observation by the prince in the male-dominated land space. Gradually, she becomes stronger and her power accumulation comes to a critical point at the end of her presence in the second space, when she is asked to kill the prince to return to the first space. Traditionally speaking, the suggestion of killing the prince arises out of the traditional oppositional notion of the male and female, which is characterized by the early feminist theory of struggling against males to win their rights. Yet, what the little mermaid did, transcends the traditional feminist displays in that they discard the oppositional view and replace it with tolerance and self-sacrifice. It is this virtue which empowers the little mermaid and paves the way for her spiritual purification.

The Second Space: Female Spiritual Space under Male Hegemony
The labelling of the second space as spiritual is due to the fact that it is characterized by spiritual symbolization and by the confrontation between the spiritual delusion of the little mermaid and harsh male hegemony enforced by the prince. It is during the confrontation that the female subjectivity of the little mermaid has gradually become mature.

From the perspective of spatial description and gender, the land space is typically male-chauvinistic. The male hegemony is shown through the depiction of the prince's palace:

> It was built of bright yellow shining stone, with long flights of marble steps, one of which reached quite down to the sea. Splendid gilded cupolas rose over the roof, and between the pillars that surrounded the whole building stood life-like statues of marble. Through the clear crystal of the lofty windows could be seen noble rooms, with costly silk curtains and hangings of tapestry; while the walls were covered with beautiful paintings which were a pleasure to look at. (75)

The grand construction of the palace is similar with the one of the Sea King. As a spatial symbol, it shows the controlling power of the prince over the land.

After entering the second space, the little mermaid is kept in the margin in the male-dominated space. Firstly, as mentioned above, she submits to the male aesthetic standard and transforms her body shape, having suffered much pain. After she is taken by the prince to the palace:

> She was very soon arrayed in costly robes of silk and muslin, and was the most beautiful creature in the palace; but she was dumb, and could neither speak nor sing. (81)

Symbolically speaking, the beauty of the little mermaid has turned her into an alienated being which is under observation and is unable to remain equal in status with the prince. The loss of voice is a particular symbol of her absence of subjectivity and female consciousness. She is thus unable to utter her own voice and express her own thoughts to anyone.

As far as her status is concerned, she is placed among the slaves and tries to please the prince by accompanying him or dancing for him with the slaves.

> The slaves next performed some pretty fairy-like dances, to the sound of beautiful music. Then the little mermaid raised her lovely white arms, stood on the tips of her toes, and glided over the floor, and danced as no one yet had been able to dance. At each moment her beauty became more revealed, and her expressive eyes appealed more directly to the heart than the songs of the slaves. (81)

In this scene, the little mermaid is placed in the same space as the slaves and her rich affection and female consciousness are suppressed. Her existence is subordinate to the prince's male consciousness and gradually drifts away from the female independent subjectivity.

At the same time, as the male governor of the land space, the prince is not consciously aware that the little mermaid should be equal with him in status. Examined from the perspective of space, it can be noticed from the spatial management of the prince over the little mermaid that he is hegemonic in his male consciousness. Having arrived at the palace, "The prince said [the little mermaid] should remain with him always, and she received permission to sleep at his door, on a velvet cushion" (81). Spatially speaking, the place the little mermaid sleeps is the margin of the prince's, which clearly shows the status difference of the two characters created by the prince. After losing her voice, the little mermaid tries to communicate with him through eye contact and dancing, yet, he fails to understand her efforts. The lack of effective communication of love leads to the prince's ignorance of the deep affection of the little mermaid and causes him to love another princess, which directly leads to the tragedy of the little mermaid. On the surface level, it seems that the tragedy arises out of her lack of voice and inability to express herself. While on the deep level, the failure of spiritual communication between them is due to the male hegemonic ideology held by the prince and the unequal status between them. It is the unreturned love which forces the little mermaid to leave the second space.

The Third Space: Transcendental Space of Female Subjectivity
The second escape is similar to the first one, which exhibits the active female consciousness of the little mermaid. The first escape is driven by the little mermaid's pursuit of love and sacrifice of her most precious physical function: her voice. The second escape causes her to sacrifice even more: her whole body. At this stage, it is more morally acceptable for her to give up killing the prince in return for her own benefits. Thus, the second escape is marked by her spiritual and moral transcending and more independent and mature individual consciousness free from gender control. The self-sufficiency of her subjectivity paves the way for her to transcend from the second space to the third one: the one which is independent and free from physical boundaries and extreme male or female hegemonic ideologies.

In contrast to common love tragedies, "The Little Mermaid" distinguishes itself by the unique female third space where the little mermaid eventually obtains independent and intact female subjectivity. In the third space, she is not only an entity existing in the space, but also a self-sufficient spatial unit.

In Soja's theory of the third space, traditional spatial research is limited within the dichotomous mode. According to him, space is not only materialistic "spatial practice", which can be standardized or labelled; also, space is not only a purely ideological sphere, a conceptualized representation of signals. Soja distinguishes space itself from spatiality and widens the geological spatial imagination and recognizes the complexity of spatial problems by introducing sociality into the study of space.

Similarly, the third space constructed by Andersen combines the features of the 'real' materialistic world of the sea and the 'imaged' female spiritual world of the land. Through combination, the third space overthrows the definition of traditional gender ideology concerning the female body, transcends the dichotomous space and builds the Other for the little mermaid, who has greatly substantiated the third space with female consciousness and enriched the text with much aesthetic beauty and vitality.

From the perspective of space, readers can not only observe the body transformation during the transcending from the sea and land space to the sky space, but also witness the mechanism of power control over the individual in the space and the efforts made by the little mermaid to fight against it. Thus, the key of aesthetic apprehension of the story does not lie in the transcending from the sea space to the land space, but in the transcending from the land space to the sky space. This breakthrough is not only a revolt against body confinement, but also a spiritual sublimation and purification of the female consciousness represented by the little mermaid.

III

To sum up, in Andersen's construction of the three spaces, the sea space highlights the materiality and objectivity of the control of female chauvinistic power, while the land space foregrounds the female spirituality in the pursuit for love. When her spirituality is marginalized, Andersen builds an independent female third space free from the limitation on body and spirit, which combines objective and subjective, concrete and abstract, tangible and intangible, physical and spiritual factors in its deconstruction as well as reconstruction of the first and second spaces. The spiritual value and significance of this transcending constitute the artistic and aesthetic essence of the story.

In the spatial analysis of "The Little Mermaid", body and gender exhibit the mechanism of power operation to readers. From the analysis above, it is safe to say that as a symbol of power control and management, the body vividly exhibits the operative mechanism of power taking effect in the space. The process of power manipulation over the little mermaid also shows her gradually maturing and independent spirit. Previous researchers have attached great importance to the exterior perspectives such as culture and myth, while failing to investigate the inner mechanisms of the text. The spatial perspective may effectively uncover the power system in the deep structure of the text, which, combined with the ideological transformation of the little mermaid, helps to reveal the hidden meaning Andersen tried to convey in this story, and helps to reveal the existence and transformation of consciousness of characters in the story.

Also, in "The Little Mermaid" the three layers of space constitute a complex web. The narration about the little mermaid in each layer is closely connected to the other two layers. The fairy tales told by Andersen is not only a transcendental representation of reality, what's more important, with its rich textual mechanism, it has turned itself into an open and dynamic space, an Andersenian "literary field", where active intertextuality has greatly enriched and empowered the characterization of the heroine and plot shaping, thus bringing novel reading experience to the readers. Different from common fairy tales, Andersen's works are not fable stories with simple allegorical connotations. Rich ideas on humanity, gender, social and moral concerns are embedded in his works. Multiple perspectives on his works will be helpful in evaluating and appreciating the complicated and abundant aesthetic connotations in the works of Hans Christian Andersen.

Paper Cutting
A Universal Language of Hans Christian Andersen

Ye Rulan
Lecturer, Research Fellow of the Nordic Literature
Research Institute, Fudan University

There once was a storyteller in Denmark who had always told tales with a piece of paper and a pair of scissors in his hands. He would fold the paper and cut it while telling his tale, then he would unfold a finished design created to his audience while the tale came to an end. Hans Christian Andersen it was, a storyteller armed with scissors and with infinite artistic and poetic inspirations. It seems that Andersen was deeply in love with paper, regarding it not merely as something to write stories on, but also as a principle component of his storytelling. He had a passion not only for words, but for images. He did not only tell and write stories, he cut stories. Although not all of his cutouts necessarily were connected to every storyline of his tales, the freehand papercuts he presented concretized some of the images in the tales, such as swans, dancers, and pierrots. In this way he verbalized his papercuts with stories, and enriched his tale-telling with visual expressions. More importantly, his papers activated the imagination of his audience, as they infused the stories with a lot of possible scenarios so that all his audiences became narrators themselves.

With the publication of Lin Hua's *Silhouetting Another H. C. Andersen* (2005) in China (see illustration 1), which brought the attention of the Chinese readers to Andersen's artistic creations of 196 examples of papercuts and sketches, the already very well-known master of fairy tales Hans Christian Andersen won a new kind of popularity as a fantastic artist among his readers. When "The Nightingale" was translated and introduced in China, Chinese readers had felt a sense of intimacy with Andersen because the story was filled with his imaginations about China. Although his nightingale was born in Denmark, the powerful wings of his story brought it all the way to the remote imperial palace in China; and now the papercuts have brought him even closer to the Chinese, as the medium of his artistic expressions generates empathic responses from them.

Illustration 1. Lin Hua: *Silhouetting Another H. C. Andersen.* 2005.

From Andersen's scissors
pops up a fairy tale;
the papercut is now yours,
the moderate judge is you.

This poem is written on one of Andersen's papercuts and manifests the great value he attached to paper cutting, which to him was "the beginning of literary creation" (Lin Hua, *Silhouetting* 55). The idea that paper cuttings carry stories in themselves is well resonated among the Chinese. As a matter of fact, paper cutting (or "Jian Zhi" in Chinese pinyin) has long been a unique art form in China and can be traced back thousands of years. As early as the Shang Dynasty (17th-11th century BC) people had used gold and silver foil, leather and silk fabric to cut and engrave decorative patterns and images. In the Western Han Dynasty (202 BC-9 AD) Emperor Wu asked a wizard to cut his favorite concubine's figure from hemp paper after she died to call back the spirit of the deceased concubine. This might be the earliest papercut in China.

After Cai Lun invented paper in the Eastern Han Dynasty (25-220 AD), the development and popularization of paper cutting as a popular art was greatly promoted. In the Song Dynasty (960-1279 AD) paper cutting developed into a decorative art on windows, lanterns, teapots, etc. By the Ming (1368-1644) and Qing (1636 1911) dynasties, the art of paper cutting had been widely practised among the common people as a vivid conveyor of folklores, folk customs, and local stories, and a visual language to express their thoughts and wishes. With the growing trend of Chinoiserie, which first emerged in France in the early 18th century and then expanded to northern Europe in the 19th century, when Hans Christian Andersen was alive, the Chinese art of paper cutting spread westward. In 2006, Chinese paper cutting was included on the list of intangible cultural heritages by the Chinese State Council (Gong Chuhan). The art of paper cutting has maintained its vitality and value in China through the ages mainly because of the profound Chinese history and culture the paper cutters have infused in it with their scissors and knives, and people are fond of this way of presentation for its liveliness and its openness to different interpretations and creative ideas. It's an art which transcends cultural and geographical boundaries, so when the Chinese readers see Hans Christian Andersen's paper cuttings they make good sense of them because the figures, pat-

Illustration 2. By Hans Christian Andersen. Odense City Museums/Hans Christian Andersen Museum.

terns and landscapes cut on paper are a universally understandable language depicting universal human themes, endowed with a strong sense of profundity and contrast.

Illustration 3. By Hans Christian Andersen. Odense City Museums/Hans Christian Andersen Museum.

Hans Christian Andersen's Papercuts vs. those of the Chinese

Chinese prefer to use red paper for their cuttings since the colour red is seen as the most auspicious colour to symbolize happiness and express blessings and wishes for a healthy, happy and long life in Chinese culture.

Illustration 4. By Hans Christian Andersen. Odense City Museums/Hans Christian Andersen Museum.

   White paper is less frequently used for cuttings because the colour white carries the connotation of inauspiciousness. Andersen's papercuts, however, are richer in colour and many of his cuts are created using white paper. When Andersen's white papercuts (or, as in illustration 2, off-white) are placed on a coloured background, the light areas present intagliated patterns that generate the power of dragging the viewer's mind all the way into the depths of the unknown world, a place to be filled in with whatever one expects. The visual effect of his coloured papercuts (see illustration 3), rather similar to that of Chinese red-paper cuttings when they are placed on a white or light-coloured background, is images in relief. One can see the patterns stand vividly revealed as if they are about to leap off the page. Thus, it is fair to say that the white-paper cuttings are the unempty empti-

Illustration 5. Sun Bird. Traditional Chinese gold foil cut.

ness that calls for the viewer to get involved and enriched, while the coloured-paper cuttings are the unfilled fullness that appeals to her and him to appreciate and accept.

With regard to the designs of patterns, it's not hard to detect that Andersen's paper cuts bear a striking resemblance to the Chinese cutouts. Apart from the symmetrical form which is the most common paper cutting design, the scenes depicted respectively by the Chinese and Danish scissors look as if they are produced under the same roof and reflect common perceptions of the world and human nature.

For instance, one of the most well-known papercuts by Andersen, the smiling sun (see illustration 4), which is now used as the logo of The

Illustrations 6 and 7. By Hans Christian Andersen. Odense City Museums/Hans Christian Andersen Museum.
Illustrations 8 and 9. Traditional Chinese papercuts. Reproduction by Sun Zhao.

Hans Christian Andersen Museum in Odense, is similar to the ancient Chinese gold foil cut "Sun Bird" (see illustration 5) – a piece of round decoration with a sun at its centre and four flying birds round it – in that both of the two works of art express the worship of the sun god. Other images and scenes appear both in Andersen and Chinese paper cuttings as well, such as stage performances, swans, and totem figures (see examples of the latter two in illustrations 6-9).

Some of Andersen's cutouts of coloured human figures (see illustrations 10-12 and the cover illustration of the present book) may remind people of Chinese shadow puppets, a special kind of Chinese papercut art that became very popular during the Tang and Song Dynasties. The Chinese shadow puppets are human figures cut from paper or animal hides with coloured paintings, their joints connected by thread so that the legs and arms can move freely in the "shadow play".

Andersen also employed the use of thread and did some needlework to create moving figures, but the difference is that Andersen's figures are mostly frontal images while the shadow puppets are in profile.

Illustrations 10, 11 and 12. Christmas Tree Ornaments. By Hans Christian Andersen. Odense City Museums/Hans Christian Andersen Museum.

Though there are several similarities between Andersen's and Chinese papercuts, Andersen's art presents distinctive features. Unlike the Chinese paper cutters, who use both scissors and knife as their tools, Andersen created all his works of art with just one pair of big scissors. It's amazing that such delicate and exquisite paper cuttings are born from that simple tool. He improvised every cutout, hence they stylistically endow a primitive simplicity. Like his fairy tales, his paper cuttings are indeed original and impressive.

He seldom cut out the details on the face of the figures. We can find similar freehand style in ancient Chinese gold and silver foil cutting, but as this art developed through time, the cutting techniques got more sophisticated and the mainstream style turned more realistic. A most important aspect of the art is how the artist deals with details, such as the eyes, facial features, the hair, and even the slightest creases in clothes, so as to achieve a true-to-life depiction of the subjects. A reader can usually get the message of the paper cutting at first glance. Whereas Andersen's papercuts are the productions of his rich fairytale imagination and his paper cutting language is more abstractly vivid and full of fantasy, and requires more efforts from the reader to savour the stories concealed in it. Just as Jens Andersen has expressed in his paper "Scissor Writing":

Illustration 13. By Hans Christian Andersen. Odense City Museums/Hans Christian Andersen Museum.

[...] we must regard Andersen's paper art: as something colourful, diverting and poetic that is extremely closely linked to his lyric poetry, drama, fairy-tales, novels and travel books. Andersen's papercuts cannot just be separated from his written oeuvre and placed beside it [...]. They belong to a world of their own, but they all have their roots in precisely the same rich, widely embracing creative imagination which in the 19th century revolutionized world literature with a long series of fairy tales told for children and for the child in every adult.

Moreover, Hans Christian Andersen excelled in paper collage. In a piece depicting four hearts and a mosque, among other things (see illustration 13), Andersen puts together several papercuts with different colors to compose a story. At the bottom of the piece, he wrote:

> Stretching their legs in delight
> they stand upon the swans holding on to the trees.
> So wonderful a comedy it seems,
> but black in colour – therefore a tragedy.

He allowed his literary language to leap off the pages, and thereby transforming it from the words sealed in print into artistic presentations. His brilliantly artistic papercuts are always a challenge to the mind because they always hold a hidden meaning and one's imagination is needed to understand them, much the same way he wrote his fairy tales.

Chinese Papercuts of Hans Christian Andersen's Fairy Tales

Hans Christian Andersen is not the only person who created papercuts for his fairy tales. In China, a young papercut artist named Lu Xue (1971-) got inspiration from Andersen and scissored a series of papercuts for each of the five Andersen stories: "The Little Mermaid", "The Emperor's New Clothes", "The Wild Swans", "The Ugly Duckling", and "The Little Match Girl". Xue thinks that European-style papercuts are "romantic" and "creations under the moon", while hers have stuck to the Chinese papercut art tradition, which she describes as "creations under the sun" (*China Daily*, 11 November, 2004). Her realistic approach presents the storylines to the readers from one papercut to another in such a detailed way that the appreciation of her papercuts is just like reading a picture-story book. She sprinkled her papercuts with strong Chinese flavours.

In "Andersen the Storyteller" she puts a Chinese kid among the young listeners. In one of the papercuts of "The Wild Swans", the princess is bathing in a pool of lotus flowers, which in China symbolizes chastity and purity. With her artistic interpretations, Lu Xue internalized Andersen's fairy tales and successfully achieved a creation with a mix of Eastern and European ideas. Her papercuts help to reestablish a link to the past, to Andersen's time, and promote the active use of it as a source of innovation.

With papercut art – a sort of universal language outside Denmark – as a carrier of Andersen's stories, his literary works will pass through time and space, and always keep recharged with life and energy as people from different countries retell his stories with his papercuts according to their understanding in the modern context, and thus inject exuberant vitality and endow Hans Christian Andersen with the power of immortality. Such cultural integration will promote the continuous prosperity of Andersen's literary achievement and foster the development of new literary and artistic creations inspired by Andersen's works.

References

Hans Christian Andersen Publications in Danish
Andersen, H. C. *Eventyr*. 1-7. By Erik Dal, Erling Nielsen, Flemming Hovmann. København: Hans Reitzels Forlag, 1963-90.
—. *Mit Livs Eventyr* [1855]. 1-2. Rev. publ. by H. Topsøe-Jensen. København: Gyldendal, 1975.
—. *Fodreise fra Holmens Canal til Østpynten af Amager i Aarene 1828-29* [1829]. København: Borgen/Det danske Sprog- og Litteraturselskab 1986.
—. *Improvisatoren* [1835]. By Mogens Brøndsted. 2. rev. publ. København: Borgen/ Det danske Sprog- og Litteraturselskab, 2004.
—. *Andersen. H. C. Andersens samlede værker*. 1-18. København: Gyldendal/ Det danske Sprog- og Litteraturselskab, 2003-2007.
—. *Mit Livs Eventyr 1855-67*. Ed. facsimile by Bruno Svindborg. 2007. http://www.kb.dk/da/kb/nb/ha/e-mss/hca_selvbiografier/collin9_4. html

Hans Christian Andersen Publications in English
Andersen, Hans Christian. *Fairytales and Other Stories by Hans Christian Andersen*. Trans. W. A. and J. K. Craigie. London: Oxford Press, 1914.
—. *The Complete Fairy Tales and Stories*. Trans. Erik Christian Haugaard. New York: Doubleday, 1974.
—. *The Fairy Tale of My Life: an Autobiography*. Republ. New introduction by Naomi Lewis. New York: Cooper Square Press, 2000.
—. *The Improvisatore: or, Life in Italy*. Trans. Mary Howitt. Reprint. Kessinger, 2004.
—. *Andersen's Fairy Tales*. Trans. Pat Shaw Iversen. London and New York: Signet Classic, 2004.
—. *Fairy Tales*, trans. Tiina Nunally. New York: Penguin Books, 2004.

Other Works Cited
Adriansen, Bent. "Debat: Den Lille Havfrue på rejse til Shanghai". *Jyllands-Posten* 2009-03-22. Debat: 18. Artikel-id: e174219a.
Allen, Amy. *The Power of Feminist Theory: Domination, Resistance, Solidarity*. Boulder, CO: Westview Press, 1999.
Andersen, Carsten A. "Den Lille Havfrue slog de nordiske lande". *Tic-travel.dk* 2010-11-08. http://www.tic.travel/ in-the-deep/08112010/ den-lille-havfrue-slog-de-nordiske-lande (2012-08-30; Anne Klara Bom).
Andersen, Jens. "Scissor Writing". *Hans Christian Andersen – Paper Cuts*. Det Kongelige Bibliotek, 2002. (http://wayback.kb.dk:8080/wayback -1.4.2/wayback/20100107153228/http://www2.kb.dk/elib/mss/hcaklip//intro-en.htm)

Andersen, Jens. *Hans Christian Andersen: A New Life.* New York: Overlook Duckworth, Peter Mayer Publishers, 2005. (《安徒生传》, 陈雪松, 刘寅龙译, 北京, 九州出版社, 2005).

Ashworth, Gregory John. "Heritage, Identity, and Places: For Tourists and Host Communities". *Tourism in Destination Communities.* Eds. Shalini Singh, Dallen J. Timothy, Ross K. Dowling. Wallingford: CABI, 2003: 79-97.

Baccolini, Raffaella. "Gender and Genre in the Feminist Critical Dystopias of Katharine Burdekin, Margret Atwood, and Octavia Butler". *Future Females, the Next Generation: New Voices and Velocities in Feminist Science Fiction Criticism.* Boston: Rowman & Littlefield Publishers, 2000: 13-34.

Barr, Marleen S., ed. *Future Females, The Next Generation: New Voices and Velocities in Feminist Science Fiction Criticism.* Boston: Rowman & Littlefield Publishers, 2000.

Barringer, Tim. "The South Kensington Museum and the colonial project". *Colonialism and the Object. Empire, Material Culture and the Museum.* Eds. Tim Barringer, Tom Flynn. London: Routledge, 1998: 11-27.

Barthes, Roland. *Image, Music, Text.* New York: Hill and Wang, 1977.

Bauer, Martin W.; Aarts, Bas. "Corpus Construction: A Principle for Qualitative Data Collection". *Qualitative Researching with Text, Image, and Sound.* Eds. Martin W. Bauer, Georg Gaskell. London: Sage, 2000: 19-37.

Benko, Georges; Strohmayer, Ulf, eds. *Space and Social Theory: Interpreting Modernity and Postmodernity.* Oxford, England; Malden, MA: Blackwell Publishers, 1997.

Bettelheim, Bruno. *The Uses of Enchantment: The Meaning and Importance of Fairy Tales.* New York: Vintage Books: A Division of Random House, Inc., 1989.

Bi Shumin. "The Constant Renewed Little Mermaid". *Reading and Writing* (《读与写》). Vol. 4, 2009.

Billig, Michael. *Talking of The Royal Family.* London: Routledge, 1992.

—. *Banal Nationalism.* London: Sage, 1995.

—. "Discursive, Rhetorical and Ideological Messages". *Discourse Theory and Practice.* Eds. Margareth Wetherell, Stephanie Taylor, Simeon J. Yates. London: Sage, 2001: 210-221.

Bloom, Harold. *Hans Christian Andersen.* New York: Chelsea House Publishing, 2004.

Bom, Anne Klara. "When Heritage Tourism goes Glocal. The Little Mermaid in Shanghai". *Hans Christian Andersen in China.* Odense: Syddansk Universitetsforlag, 2014 (in the present book. Also published in *Journal of Heritage Tourism*, Vol. 7, No. 4. Taylor & Francis, 2012).

Bramsen, Christopher Bo. "Kronik: Den Lille Havfrue på Kina-tur". *Jyllands-Posten* 2010-03-25. Debat: 26. Artikel-id: e1f0ffda.

Brandes, Georg. *Samlede Skrifter* 1-17. København: Gyldendal, 1899-1906.

Bredsdorff, Elias. *Hans Christian Andersen: The Story of His Life and work, 1805-75*. London: Phaidon, 1975.

Brown, Maria. "Representing the Body of a Nation: The Art Exhibitions of New Zealand's National Museum". *Third Text*. 2002 (16:3): 285-294.

Bøggild, Jacob. *Svævende stasis: Arabesk og allegori i H. C. Andersens eventyr og historier*. København: Spring, 2012.

Cao Wenxuan. *Journal of Hunan Science and Technology College* (《湖南科技学院学报》). March 2006 (27:3).

Chen Bochui. "What We Should Learn from Andersen". *Andersen Research in China for One Hundred Years*. Ed. Wang Quangen. Beijing: China Peace Publishing House, 2005: 69-74.

Chen Liang. "Gender, Body, and Space: a Spatial Analysis of 'The Little Mermaid'". *Hans Christian Andersen in China*. Odense: Syddansk Universitetsforlag, 2014 (in the present book).

Cheng Kaicheng; Ying Zhaohua. "Love is the Transcendence of Death: the death consciousness in Andersen's fairy tales". *Journal of Southeast Guizhou National Teachers College*. 2002 (5): 69-70.

Chuban guangjiao (Wide Angle of Publications) 8, 1999.

Cixous, Helene. "The Laugh of the Medusa". *Signs*. The University of Chicago Press. 1976 (1:4): 875-893.

Cravens, Gwyneth. "Review of 'The Little Mermaid'". *Nation*. 1992 (254:18): 638-640.

Dahlerup, Pil. "'Litter Mermaid' Deconstructed". *Scandinavian Studies*. Autumn 1990 (62.4): 418-428. Rpt. in *Short Story Criticism*. Ed. Janet Witalec. Vol. 56. Detroit: Gale, 2003. (*Literature Resource Center*. Web. 2012-08 01; Lu Li'an).

—. "Splash! Six Views of 'The Little Mermaid'". *Scandinavian Studies*. 1991 (63:2): 141-162.

Detering, Heinrich. "The Phoenix Principle: Some Remarks on H. C. Andersen's Poetological Writings". *Hans Christian Andersen: A Poet in Time*. Ed. Johan de Mylius. The Hans Christian Andersen Center, Odense University, Odense University Press, 1999: 51-65.

Dollerup, Cay. "Translation as a Creative Force in Literature: the Birth of the European Bourgeois Fairy Tale". *The Modern Language Review*. 1995 (90:1): 94-102.

Easterlin, Nancy. "Hans Christian Andersen's Fish Out of Water". *Philosophy and Literature*. 2001 (25:2): 251-277.

Elleström, Lars. *Divine Madness: On Interpreting Literature, Music and the Visual Arts*. Bucknell University Press, 2002.

Fang Weiping. *Theory of Chinese Children's Literature: A History*. Shanghai: Publishing House for Teens and Children, 2007. (方卫平,《中国儿童文学理论发展史》, 上海, 少年儿童出版社, 2007).

Farquhar, Mary Ann. *Children's Literature in China: From Lu Xun to Mao Zedong*. Armonk, NY: M. E. Sharpe, 1999.

Frandsen, Johs. Nørregaard. "The Writer of Tales: Hans Christian Andersen as a Cultural Bridge-Builder". *Forum for World Literature Studies*. 2011 (2). (*Literature Resource Center*. Web. 2012-08-01; Lu Li'an).

Frandsen, Line. "– Hvor har vi savnet dig". *BT* 2010-11-20. Artikel-id: e24d98ec.

Frank, Diane Crone and Jeffrey. "The Real Hans Christian Andersen". *The Stories of Hans Christian Andersen*. Trans. Diane Crone Frank, Jeffrey Frank. Boston: Houghton Mifflin, 2003: 1-14.

Frausing, Mikael. "Er Den Lille Havfrue et dansk nationalsymbol?" *danmarkshistorien.dk* 2011-08-18. http:// www.tic.travel/in-the-deep/08112010/den-lille-havfrue-slog-de-nordiske-lande (2012:08-30; Anne Klara Bom).

Frow, John. "Cultural property". *Handbook of Cultural Analysis*. Eds. Tony Bennett, John Frow. London: Sage, 2008: 427-446.

Gems, Pam. *Hans Christian Andersen's The Little Mermaid*. London: Oberon, 2004.

Gjerløff, Martin. "Den Lille Havfrue i vand til halsen". *Erhvervsbladet* 2009-02-12. Opinion: 2. Artikel-id: e16756b0.

Gong Chuhan. *Paper Cutting*. Beijing: The Publishing House of the China Literary Federation, 2008.

Goul, Nanna. "Kommentar: H. C. Andersens kinesiske fanklub". *Weekendavisen* 2010-06-18. Bøger: 16. Artikel-id: e20fe470.

Graham, Brian; Ashworth, Gregory J.; Tunbridge, John E. *A Geography of Heritage: Power, Culture, and Economy*. London: Arnold, 2000.

Grønbech, Jens. "Den Lille Havfrue skal reddes fra kulden". *Newspaq* 2010-03-05. Artikel-id: e1e95899.

Gu Junzheng. "H. C. Andersen: A Biography". *Fiction Monthly*. August 1925 (16:8).

Guo Dehua. "What Can We Chinese Learn from Hans Christian Andersen?" *Andersen og Verden (Andersen and the World). Indlæg fra den første internationale H. C. Andersen-konference: 25.-31. august 1991*. Eds. Johan de Mylius, Aage Jørgensen, Viggo Hjørnager Pedersen. H. C. Andersen Centret, Odense Universitet, Odense Universitetsforlag, 1993: 346-52.

Guo Yanli. *A Brief Introduction to Modern Chinese Literary Translation*. Wuhan: Hubei Education Press, 1998.

Habegger, Alfred. *Gender, Fantasy, and Realism in American Literature*. New York: Columbia University Press, 1982.

Hagmund, Peter. "Send Andersen til Kina". *Fyens Stiftstidende* 2009-04-16. Artikel-id: e17b9e4d.

Halgreen, Troels. "Havfrue: Den lille havfrue stikker til søs". *Information* 2009-02-04. 1. sektion: 16-17. Artikel-id: e16474cd.

Han Jin. "The journey of various versions of Andersen's fairy tales in China over the century". *China Reading Weekly,* March 23, 2005. (韩进,《安徒生童话在中国的百年版本之旅》,《中华读书报》2005-03-23).

Hansen, Jørgen Bülow. "Debat: Havfruen bli'r her". *Ekstra Bladet* 2009-09-17. Nationen: 21. Artikel-id: e1727256.

Hasse, Donald. "Feminist Fairytale Scholarship". *Fairy Tales and Feminism: New Approaches.* Ed. Donald Hasse. Detroit: Wayne State University Press, 2004: 1-36.

Hoffmann, E. T. A.: *Der goldne Topf.* Projekt Gutenberg: http://www.gutenberg.org/ files/17362/17362-h/17362-h.htm.

Holm, Anette. "Ok, havfruen skal ud at rejse". *Dagbladet Ringkøbing-Skjern* 2009-03-17. Videbæk: 14. Artikel-id: e1730ce2.

Humphrey, Caroline; Verdery, Katherine. "Introduction: Raising Questions about Property". *Property in Question: Value Transformations in the Global Economy.* Eds. Katherine Verdery, Caroline. Humphrey. Oxford: Berg Publishers, 2004: 1-25.

Hu Shi. "Constructive Literary Revolution: A Literature National Speech". *Sources of Chinese Tradition, Vol.2.* Eds. Wing-tsit Chan, Joseph Adler. New York: Columbia University Press, 2000: 361-363.

—. "The Chinese Renaissance". *Selected Works of Hu Shi.* Ed. Ouyang Zhesheng, Liu Hongzhong. Shanghai: Foreign Language Teaching and Research Press, 2000.

Huang Jigang. "Analysis on Spatial Cultural Theory". *Xinjiang Social Science.* 2008 (5): 7-79.

Ingham, Herbert S. *The Theory of Space.* Roslyn Estates, N.Y., 1955.

Ingwersen, Niels. "Andersen after 2005: Will it Ever End? On Four Recent Volumes on the Tales of Hans Christian Andersen". *Scandinavian Studies.* 2007 (79:4): 489 ff. (*Literature Resource Center.* Web. 2011-10-19; Lu Li'an).

Jackson, Rosemary. *Fantasy: The Literature of Subversion.* London: Methuen, 1981.

Jameson, Fredric; Miyoshi, Masao, ed. *Cultures of Globalization.* Durham and London: Duke University Press, 1998.

Jenkins, Richard. *Being Danish. Paradoxes of Identity in Everyday Life.* Copenhagen: Museum Tusculanum Press, 2011.

Jensen, Martin Kjær. "En, to, tre – det er en prøve". *BT* 2010-03-25. Nyheder: 25. Artikel-id: e1f1142f.

Kofoed, Niels: "The Arabesque and the Grotesque". *Hans Christian Andersen. A Poet in Time.* Eds. Johan de Mylius et al. Odense: Odense University Press 1999.

—. *Arabesken og dens æstetiske former.* København: C. A. Reitzel 1999.

Kruhøffer, Annette. "Men de behandler hende godt". *Østerbro Avis* 2010-05-10. Artikel-id: e2016ba0.

Lan Shouting; Chen Ying. "On Tragic Consciousness in Andersen's Fairytales". *Journal of Heihe*, 2007 (3): 40-42.

Larsen, Hans. "Drager kan erstatte havfruen". *Berlingske Tidende* 18. februar 2009. Indland: 10. Artikel-id: e16916aa.

Lefebvre, Henri. *The Production of Space.* Trans. Donald Nicholson Smith. Oxford UK: Blackwell Ltd., 1991.

—. "Reflections on the Politics of Space". *Radical Geography.* Ed. Richard Peet. London: Methuen 1978.

Lefevere, Andre. *Translation, Rewriting and Manipulation of Literary Fame*. Shanghai: Shanghai Foreign Language Education Press, 2004.

Lennox, Charlotte. *The Female Quixote*. Oxford University Press, 1989.

Li Changzhong. "Dilemma of Temporal Narration and Significance of the Emergence of Spatial Theory". *Journal of Xianyang Teachers College*. 2008 (1): 64-69.

Li Hongye. "Serious Insufficiency Reflected by Realistic ideology – Andersen's Fairy Tales from the Early 1930s to before the Founding of PRC". *Social Science Journal of Xiangtan University*, 2002 (26:2): 69-72. (李红叶，现实观照下的严重缺失——安徒生童话在30年代初至建国前,《湘潭大学社会科学学报》, 2002 (26:2): 69-72).

—. "On the Evolvement of the Children's Spirit of Anderson's Fairy Tales". *Journal of Loudi Teachers College*, 2002 (1), 34-38. (李红叶，论安徒生童话"儿童精神"的流变,《娄底师专学报》2002 (1): 34-38).

—. *Chinese Interpretations of Andersen's Fairy Tales*. Beijing: China Peace Publishing House, 2005. (李红叶,《安徒生童话的中国阐释》, 北京, 中国和平出版社, 2005).

Lieberman, Marcia R. "'Some Day My Prince Will Come': Female Acculturation through the Fairy Tale". *College English*. Dec., 1972 (34:3): 383-395.

Lin Hua. *Silhouetting Another Hans Christian Andersen*. Beijing: SDX Joint Publishing Company, 2005.

—, translator. *A Picture Book without Pictures*. Shanghai: Shanghai Social Science Institute Press, 2005.

Liu Jin. "Western Spatial Theory and Literary Ideas Since the Middle and Late 20th Century". *Research on Literary Theories*. 2007 (6): 19-25.

Lurie, Alison. "The Underduckling: Hans Christian Andersen". *Boys and Girls Forever: Children's Classics from Cinderella to Harry Potter*. New York: Penguin Books, 2003: 1-11. Rpt. In *Children's Literature Review*. Ed. Tom Burns. Detroit: Gale, 2006 (113). (*Literature Resource Center*. Web. 2011-10-18; Lu Li'an).

Mai, Anne-Marie. "'The Dryad' by Hans Christian Andersen: a Fairy Tale on Modern Times and the World Exhibition of 1867". *Forum for World Literature Studies*. 2011 (3:2): 211 ff. (*Literature Resource Center*. Web. 2012-08-01; Lu Li'an).

Maine, H.S. *Ancient law*. Tuscon: University of Arizona Press, 1986/1963.

Meng Zhaoyi; Li Zaidong. Eds. *History of Chinese Literary Translation*. Beijing: Peking University Press, 2005.

Moi, Toril. *Sexual/Textual Politics: Feminist literary Theory*. London and New York: Methuen, 1985.

Moko Mead, Sidney (ed.). *Te Maori*. New York: Harry N. Abrams, 1984.

Mortensen, Finn Hauberg. "The Little Mermaid: icon and disneyfication". *Scandinavian Studies*. 2008 (80:4): 437 ff. (*Literature Resource Center*. Web. 2011-10-18; Lu Li'an).

Mulvey, Laura. "Visual Pleasure and Narrative Cinema". *Screen*. Autumn, 1975 (16:3): 6-18.

Munk, Jens Peter. Private email, 2012-01-30 (Anne Klara Bom).

Mylius, Johan de, ed. *Hans Christian Andersen: A Poet in Time*. The Hans Christian Andersen Center, Odense: Odense University Press, 1999.

—; Nunnally, Tiina. "Hans Christian Andersen". *Danish Writers from the Reformation to Decadence, 1550-1900*. Ed. Marianne Stecher-Hansen. Detroit: Gale, 2004. *Dictionary of Literary Biography*, Vol. 300. (*Literature Resource Center*. Web. 2011-10-18; Lu Li'an).

—. "'Our Time is the Time of the Fairy Tale': Hans Christian Andersen between Traditional Craft and Literary Modernism". *Marvels & Tales*. 2006 (20:2): 166 ff. (*Literature Resource Center*. Web. 2011-10-19; Lu Li'an).

Nielsen, Gert Holmgaard. "Lille havfrue, stor redningsmand". *Politiken* 2010-08-13. Kultur: 7. Artikel-id: e222934c.

Olsen, Nis; Nielsen, Jakob. "Havfruen er klar til Kinarejsen". *Politiken* 2009-02-21. Artikel-id: e16a7e37.

Pan Yan (潘延). "Andersen in China: Reflections on Andersen Studies". (《安徒生在中国——对安徒生研究的回顾与反思》). *Journal of Railway Teacher's College* (《铁道师院学报》). 1997 (6).

Pettit, Stephen. "Is He Worth It?" *Spectator* (298.9229). 2005-06-25. 55-56. Rep. in *Children's Literature Review*. Ed. Tom Burns. Detroit: Gale, 2006 (113:m). (*Literature Resource Center*. Web. 2012-08-01; Lu Li'an).

Pieterse, Jan Nederveen. "Multiculturalism and Museums: Discourse about Others in the Age of Globalization". *Theory, Culture, and Society*. 1997 (14): 123-146.

Poria, Yaniv; Butler, Richard W.; Airey, David. "The Core of Heritage Tourism". *Annals of Tourism Research*. 2003 (30:1): 238-254.

Posey, Darrell. "Can Cultural Rights Protect Traditional Cultural Knowledge and Biodiversity?". *Cultural Rights and Wrongs*. Ed. Halina Nieć. Paris: UNESCO, 1998: 42-56.

Qian Zhongli. "Religious Connotation in Andersen's Fairy Tales". *Journal of Foreign Language Studies, PLA*. 2009 (32:4): 99-102. (钱中丽，安徒生童话中的宗教意蕴,《解放军外国语学院学报》，2009 (32:4): 99-102).

—. "Andersen's Fairy Tales in the Mid-20th Century Chinese Context". *Foreign Literature Studies*, 2011 (1): 144-150. (钱中丽, 20世纪中叶中国语境下的安徒生童话,《外国文学研究》2011(1), 144-150).

Ritzaus Bureau. "Havfruen tilbage – men kun på storskærm". *Ritzaus Bureau*. 2010-04-29. Artikel-id: e1fdb37c.

Robertson, Roland. "Glocalization: Time-space and homogeneity-heterogeneity". *Global modernities*. Eds. Mike Featherstone, Scott Lash, Roland Robertson. London: Sage, 1995: 25-45.

Roest-Madsen, Lars. "Havfruen skal få kineserne til at cykle". *Metro Express* 2010-02-23. Indland: 10. Artikel-id: e1e54b04.

Ross, Deborah. "Escape from Wonderland: Disney and the Female Imagination". *Marvels & Tales*. 2004 (18:1): 53-66. Rpt. in *Children's Literature Review*. Ed. Tom Burns. Detroit: Gale, 2009 (143). (*Literature Resource Center*. Web. 2012-08-28; Lu Li'an).

Rossel, Sven Hakon. *"Do You Know the Land, Where the Lemon Trees Bloom"? Hans Christian Andersen and Italy.* Roma: Edizioni Nuova Cultura, 2009.

Rowlands, Michael. "Cultural Rights and Wrongs: Uses of the Concept of Property". *Property in Question: Value Transformations in the Global Economy.* Eds. Katherine Verdery, Caroline Humphrey. Oxford: Berg Publishers, 2004: 207-226.

Rytgaard, Nikolaj. "Slipsefolket følger efter Den Lille Havfrue". *Berlingske Tidende* 2010-04-09. Business: 13. Artikel-id: e1f5ac39.

Schauser, Søren. "Portræt: Den Lille Havfrue bortføres". *Berlingske Tidende* 2010-03-25. Bagsiden: 12. Artikel-id: e1f11d4e.

Schlegel, Friedrich: "Brief über den Roman". http://www.literaturwelt.com/werke/schlegel_friedrich/romanbrief.html.

Schwab, Gabriele. *The Mirror and the Killer Queen: Otherness in Literary Language.* Bloomington: Indiana University Press, 1996.

Shi Qin'e. *H. C. Andersen's Fairy Tales.* Beijing: China Pictorial Press, 2012.

Showalter, Elaine. *Sister's Choice: Tradition and Change in Women's Writing.* New York: Oxford University Press, 1991.

Spacks, Patricia Meyer. *The Female Imagination.* New York: Knopf, 1975.

Sun Yuxiu. "Review of Famous European and American Novels". (《读欧美名家小说札记》),《东方杂志》, 1909 年第 6 卷第 1 号"文苑"栏目.

—. "Adventure, Spirit and Monster Stories" (《神怪小说》). *Fiction Monthly* (《小说月报》). 1913 (8).

—. "The Writer of Adventure, Spirit and Monster Stories and His Masterpieces" (《神怪小说之著者及其杰作》). *Fiction Monthly.* 1913 (10).

Tang Jun; Yang Tianshu. "Analysis of Literary Stereotypes in Andersen's *The Little Mermaid*". *Journal of Xiangtan Teachers College.* 2001 (6): 86-90.

Tatar, Maria. *The Annotated Hans Christian Andersen.* Edited with an Introduction and Notes by Maria Tatar. New York: W. W. Norton & Company, 2008.

Thacker, Deborah Cogan and Jean Webb. *Introducing Children's Literature.* London and New York: Routledge, 2002.

Theatre and Opera in China. "Transformation from the Ugly Duckling to the White Swan: Congratulations on the 40th Anniversary of the Foundation of Xi'an Children's Art Theatre (《从丑小鸭到白天鹅 ——贺西安儿童艺术院40年》)". (《中国戏剧》). 1999 (9).

Timothy, Dallen J.; Boyd, Stephen. "Heritage tourism in the 21st century: Valued traditions and new perspectives". *Journal of Heritage Tourism.* (1:1): 1-16.

UNESCO. "Convention Concerning the Protection of the World Cultural and Natural Heritage". <http://whc.unesco.org/en/conventiontext>.

UNESCO. "What is Intangible Cultural Heritage?". <http://www.unesco.org/culture/ich/index.php?lg=en&pg=00002>.

Vergo, Peter (ed.). *The new museology.* London: Reaktion Books, 1989.

Vesterberg, Henrik. "Hvad var det hun ville?". *Politiken* 2010-03-26. Kultur: 1. Artikel-id: e1f17434.

Walker, Nancy A. *Feminist Alternatives: Irony and Fantasy in the Contemporary Novels by Women*. Jackson, Miss.: University Press of Mississippi, 1990.

Wang Aiping. "Fantasy, Irony & Autonomy: A Feminist Transcoding of 'The Little Mermaid'". *Hans Christian Andersen in China*. Odense: Syddansk Universitetsforlag, 2014 (in the present book).

Wang Lei. *Andersen's Fairy tales and China's Modern Children's Literature*. Shanghai: South-East Normal University Press, 2009. (王蕾,《安徒生童话与中国现代儿童文学》，上海，华东师范大学出版社，2009).

Wang Quangen. *Zhongguo xiandai ertongwenxue wenlun xuan* (Collected essays on modern Chinese children's literature). Guilin: Guangxi Renmin Chubanshe (Guangxi people's publishing House): 1989.

—. *New Thoughts in Contemporary Chinese Children's Literature*. Chongqing: Chongqing Publishing House, 2000.

—. *Andersen Research in China for One Hundred Years*. Beijing: China Peace Publishing House, 2005. (王泉根,《中国安徒生研究一百年》，北京，中国和平出版社，2005).

—. "Break-through of Children's Literary Studies: A Preface." Preface to *In the Wonderland of Fairy Tale: New Perspective of Chinese and Western Fairy Tale Literature*, Shu Wei. Beijing: Foreign Teaching and Research Publishing House, 2011, 1. (王泉根，"童话研究的突破性成果"，舒伟,《走进童话奇境——中西童话文学新论》，北京，外语教学与研究出版社，2011).

Weiner, Annette B. *Inalienable Possessions*. Berkeley: University of California Press, 1992.

West-Pavlov, Russell. *Space in Theory: Kristeva, Foucault, Deleuze / Russel West-Pavlov*. Amsterdam: Rodopi, 2009.

Winge, Mette. "H. C. Andersen ville elske havfruebog". *Politiken* 2010-03-01. Artikel-id: e1e7b61b.

Woolf, Virginia. *A Room of One's Own*. Oxford University Press, 1992.

Wu Qinan. *History of Chinese Fairy Tale*. Shanghai: Publishing House for Teens and Children, 2007. (吴其南,《中国童话发展史》，上海，少年儿童出版社，2007).

Wullschlager, Jackie. *Hans Christian Andersen: The Life of a Storyteller*. Chicago: University of Chicago Press, 2002.

Xie Na. Spatial Production and Literary Representation. Beijing: China People University Press, 2010.

Yan Wenjing. "Postcript to *Nannan and the Beard Uncle*". *A Collection of Yan Wenjing's Fables and Fairy Tales*. (《严文井童话寓言集》). The People's Literature Press (北京，人民文学出版社).

Yan Xiaojiang. "On the Role of Ideology in Translation Practice." *US-China Foreign Language*. 2007 (5:4): 63-65.

Yang Ning. "Singing across Time and Space: Modern Consciousness in Andersen's *Ugly Duck* and *The Little Mermaid*". *Journal of Guizhou Southern Teachers College*. 2004 (5): 65-67.

Ye Junjian. "The Preface to Selections of Andersen's Fairy Tales in 1958". *Andersen Research in China for One Hundred Years*. Ed. Wang Quangen. Beijing: China Peace Publishing House, 2005: 83-92.

—. "Preface to *A Complete Andersen*". *A Complete Andersen*. Trans. Ye Junjian. Beijing: Qinghua University Press, 1999.

Ye Rulan. Private email, 2011-12-17 (Anne Klara Bom).

—. "Hans Christian Andersen in China: An Overview". *Hans Christian Andersen in China*. Odense: Syddansk Universitetsforlag, 2014 (in the present book).

—. "Paper Cutting: A Universal Language of Hans Christian Andersen". *Hans Christian Andersen in China* Odense: Syddansk Universitetsforlag, 2014 (in the present book).

Ye Shengtao. "The Emperor's New Clothes". *Education Magazine* (《教育杂志》). 1930 (22:1).

Yenika-Agbaw, Vivian. "Reading disability in children's literature: Hans Christian Andersen's tales". *Journal of Literary & Cultural Disability Studies*. (Jan. 2011 (5:1): 91-97. (*Literature Resource Center*. Web. 2012-08-01; Lu Li'an).

Zhang Xiaofeng. "The Intimate Topic From the Age of 5 to 55" (《5岁到55岁的亲密话题》). *Young Writers Journal* (《小作家选刊》), 2005 (4).

Zhao Jingshen. "Criticism on Fairy Tales". Shanghai New Culture Book Society. March, 1922.

Zhao Lingli (赵伶俐). "New Exploration of Andersen's Fairy Tale Art". (《安徒生童话艺术新探》). *Journal of Zhejiang Normal Institute* (《浙江师范学院学报》). 1984 (2).

Zheng Jinhuai. "Who first introduced Andersen to the Chinese readers?" *Reading*. 2009 (12): 95-97. (郑锦华,《谁最早向中国读者介绍安徒生》,《博览群书》2009 (2)).

Zheng Zhenduo. *Literature Compendium*. Guilin: Guangxi Normal University Press, 2003.

—. "Preface to H. C. Andersen Special Edition". *Fiction Monthly*. August, 1925 (16:8).

Zhou Gang. *Language, Myth, Identity: The Chinese Vernacular Movement in a Comparative Perspective*. PhD Thesis. Davis: University of California, 2003.

Zhou Shoujuan. *A Collection of European Short Stories* (《欧美名家短篇小说丛刊》). Beijing: Zhonghua Book Company, 1917 (2).

"Zhou Zuoren". *Wikipedia: The Free Encyclopedia*. Wikimedia Foundation, Inc. 2014-01-31. (Web. 2014-02-08; Zhu Jianxing).

Zhou Zuoren. "A Brief Remark on Fairy Tales". *Monthly Magazine of Ministry of Education Editorial Department*. September, 1913.

—. "A Biography of the Danish Poet Hans Christian Andersen". *Ruo Club Periodical*. December, 1913 (1). (周作人,《丹麦诗人安兑尔然传》,《叒社丛刊》创刊号).
—. "Random Thoughts". *Le Jeunesse*, 1918 (5:3).
Zhu Liyuan. *Contemporary Western Literary Theory*. Shanghai: East China Teachers University Press, 2005.
Zipes, Jack David. "Hans Christian Andersen". *European Writers. The Romantic Century*. Ed. George Stade. New York: Charles Scribner's Sons, 1985 (6). (*Scribner Writers Series*. Web. 2011-10-18; Lu Li'an).
—. *Hans Christian Andersen: The Misunderstood Storyteller*. New York: Routledge, 2005.
—. "Critical Reflections about Hans Christian Andersen, the Failed Revolutionary". *Marvels & Tales* 2006 (20:2). (*Literature Resource Center*. Web. 2011-10-18; Lu Li'an).
—. "Hans Christian Andersen and the Discourse of the Dominated". *Fairy Tales and the Art of Subversion*. New York and London: Routledge, 2006: 81-103.

Bio Notes

Johs. Nørregaard Frandsen. Professor, Head of the Hans Christian Andersen Center, University of Southern Denmark.

Sun Jian. Professor, Director of the Nordic Literature Research Institute, Fudan University.

Torben Grøngaard Jeppesen. Museum Director, Odense City Museums; Affiliate Research Professor, Faculty of Humanities, University of Southern Denmark.

Lu Li'an. Professor, Research Fellow of the Nordic Literature Research Institute, Fudan University.

Jacob Bøggild. Professor, the Hans Christian Andersen Center, University of Southern Denmark.

Li Hongye. Guest Professor at the Hans Christian Andersen Center, from the Department of Chinese Language and Literature, Hunan University of Humanities, Science and Technology.

Zhu Jianxin. Associate Professor, Research Fellow of the Nordic Literature Research Institute, Fudan University.

Wang Aiping. Associate Professor, Research Fellow of the Nordic Literature Research Institute, Fudan University.

Chen Liang. Associate Professor, Research Fellow of the Nordic Literature Research Institute, Fudan University.

Ye Rulan. Lecturer, Research Fellow of the Nordic Literature Research Institute, Fudan University.

Anne Klara Bom. PhD, the Hans Christian Andersen Center, University of Southern Denmark.